St. Martin
St. Barts

Fourth Edition

Pascale Couture

Travel better, enjoy more
ULYSSES
Travel Guides

Offices

U.S.A.: Ulysses Travel Guides, 305 Madison Avenue, Suite 1166, New York, NY 10165, ☎ 1-877-542-7247, info@ulysses.ca, www.ulyssesguides.com

CANADA: Ulysses Travel Guides, 4176 St. Denis Street, Montréal, Québec, H2W 2M5, ☎ (514) 843-9447 or 1-877-542-7247, ⇄(514) 843-9448, info@ulysses.ca, www.ulyssesguides.com

EUROPE: Les Guides de Voyage Ulysse SARL, BP 159, 75523 Paris Cedex 11, France, ☎ 01 43 38 89 50, ⇄01 43 38 89 52, voyage@ulysse.ca, www.ulyssesguides.com

Distributors

U.S.A.: The Globe Pequot Press, 246 Goose Lane, Guilford, CT 06437 - 0480, ☎1-800-243-0495, Fax: 800-820-2329, sales@globe-pequot.com

CANADA: Ulysses Books & Maps, 4176 St. Denis Street, Montréal, Québec, H2W 2M5, ☎ (514) 843-9882, ext.2232, 800-748-9171, Fax: 514-843-9448, info@ulysses.ca, www.ulyssesguides.com

GREAT BRITAIN AND IRELAND: World Leisure Marketing, Unit 11, Newmarket Court, Newmarket Drive, Derby DE24 8NW, ☎ 1 332 57 37 37, Fax: 1 332 57 33 99, office@wlmsales.co.uk

SCANDINAVIA: Scanvik, Esplanaden 8B, 1263 Copenhagen K, DK, ☎ (45) 33.12.77.66, Fax: (45) 33.91.28.82

SWITZERLAND: OLF, P.O. Box 1061, CH-1701 Fribourg, ☎ (026) 467.51.11, Fax: (026) 467.54.66

OTHER COUNTRIES: Contact Ulysses Books & Maps, 4176 St. Denis Street, Montréal, Québec, H2W 2M5, ☎ (514) 843-9882, ext.2232, ☎ 800-748-9171, Fax: 514-843-9448, info@ulysses.ca, www.ulyssesguides.com

Cataloguing-in-Publication Data (see p 6)
 Printed in Canada
ISBN 2-89464-369-1

I hope that
succeeding generations will be able
to be idle...
that they may rest
by the sea and dream...

The Story of My Heart
Richard Jefferies

Author
Pascale Couture

Project Coordinator
Stéphane G. Marceau

Copy Editing
Jacqueline Grekin
Editing Assistance
Eileen Connolly

Translation
Danielle Gauthier

Cartographer
Patrick Thivierge

Photography
Cover page
Image Bank
Inside pages
Lorette Pierson
Claude Hervé-Bazin

Computer Graphics
André Duchesne

Artistic Director
Patrick Farei (Atol)

Illustrations
Lorette Pierson
Marie-Annick Viatour
Vincent Desruisseaux

The author thanks: Benoit Prieur; Denis Codère and Manon Bélanger (Air Transat); Élise Magras (St. Barts Tourist Office), Rollina Bridgewater and Maryse Romney (St. Martin Tourist Office).

Ulysses Travel Guides thanks: The Government of Canada, for providing financial support for our publishing activities through the Book Publishing Industry Development Program (BPIDP). We would also like to thank the Québec government—SODEC income tax program for book publication.

We value your comments, corrections and suggestions, as they allow us to keep each guide up to date. The best contributions will be rewarded with a free book from Ulysses Travel Guides. All you have to do is write us at the following address and indicate which title you would be interested in receiving (see the list at the end of the guide).

Ulysses Travel Guides

305 Madison Avenue
Suite 1166, New York
NY 10165

4176 St. Denis Street
Montréal, Québec
Canada H2W 2M5

www.ulyssesguides.com
text@ulysses.ca

Table of Contents

List of Maps

Map Symbols

❶	Tourist information	⊔	Fortress
✈	Airport	▲	Mountain
🚌	Bus station	◐	Beach
🚢	Passenger ferry	✉	Post office
H	Hospital	†	Church

Cataloguing-in-Publication Data

St. Martin, St. Barts

(Ulysses Due South)
Includes Index.
ISSN 1486-2344
ISBN 2-89464-369-1

I. Series

F2103.C6813 917.297'604 C99-301344-9

Symbols

	Ulysses's favourite
☎	Telephone number
⇄	Fax number
≡	Air conditioning
⊗	Fan
≈	Pool
ℜ	Restaurant
⊛	Whirlpool
ℝ	Refrigerator
K	Kitchenette
⌂	Sauna
⊘	Fitness centre
tv	Television
bkfst incl.	Breakfast included

ATTRACTION CLASSIFICATION

★	Interesting
★★	Worth a visit
★★★	Not to be missed

HOTEL CLASSIFICATION

Prices in this guide are for one room, double occupancy in high season, unless otherwise indicated.

RESTAURANT CLASSIFICATION

$	less than 60 F
$$	60 F to 125 F
$$$	125 F to 200 F
$$$$	more than 200 F

$	less than US$10
$$	US$10 to US$20
$$$	US$20 to US$30
$$$$	more than US$30

The prices in this guide are for a meal for one person, not including drinks and tip, unless otherwise indicated.

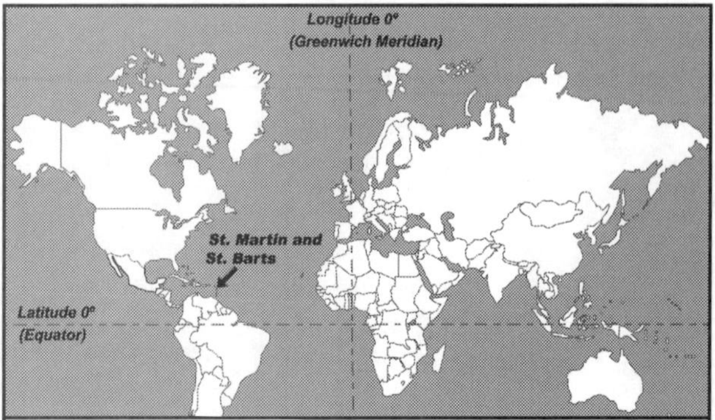

©ULYSSES

Where are St. Martin and St. Barts?

Island of St. Martin		Island of St. Barts	
Territory divided between France (Saint-Martin) and the Netherlands (Sint Maarten)		Overseas French Department	
Main Cities:	Philipsburg and Marigot	**Main City:**	Gustavia
Languages:	French, English and Dutch	**Language:**	French
Population:	69,000 inhabitants	**Population:**	6,500 inhabitants

Portrait

Orient Bay, Long Bay, Oyster Pond, Anse de Grande Saline... so many beaches conjuring up dazzling sunshine beaming down on azure waves, fine sand caressing feet, waves gently lapping the shore, the sea breeze... a symphony for the senses inviting pleasurable idleness.

St. Martin and St. Barts, the two islets at the northern tip of the Lesser Antilles archipelago, have been popular destinations at various points in history. Arawak-speaking aboriginals were undoubtedly the first to settle here over 3,500 years ago. These people, who had this peaceful land to themselves for centuries, were later followed by successive waves of immigrants from South America. The next people to land on these islands were Europeans, who, in the space of less than two centuries, became their sole rulers.

French and Dutch colonists gradually settled here, but, instead of finding the abundance they had hoped for, found themselves cultivating a barren land. For decades, nature proved a dauntless foe; intense sun and hurricanes were the cause of much hardship. Having eventually abandoned hope of cultivating anything here, residents had to wait until the beginning of the 1980s before they managed to derive any benefit from nature. Today, the idyllic beaches and shimmering waves of this barren, untamed land draw thousands of visitors every year.

Geography

Composed of over a hundred islets set in the sea like a long string of pearls, the Lesser Antilles archipelago was formed several million years ago by the movement of tectonic plates. In fact, an upsurge of magma had then driven the Atlantic plate toward the coast of the Americas. Embedding itself beneath the smaller Caribbean plate, this plate caused a host of little islands to emerge: the Lesser Antilles.

Lying at the northern extremity of this archipelago, St. Martin is an arid island. Hillsides rising from the centre of this island are covered in sparse vegetation, comprised of shrubs and cacti. Its landscape is also distinguished by long, crescent-shaped beaches punctuated by a few lianas and sea-grape trees, as well as great salt-water ponds (Simson Bay Lagoon, Great Salt Pond). These salt marshes, which have been exploited since the onset of colonization, were formed as sediment was deposited at the mouth of torrential rivers (in which the volume of sediment is particularly high during cyclonic floods), thus creating long coastal ribbons of sand and closing off large lagoons.

Barely 30km south of St. Martin, the island of St. Barts emerges from the waters, a small mountainous mass with a surface area of no more than 25km^2. Mountains form the heart of this land, where twisting roads wind their way up to a series of villages. The villages' few houses are charmingly-kept and surrounded by stunted vegetation that strains to grow in the poor volcanic soil, bereft of both lakes and rivers. The island's terrain is similar to that of St. Martin's, with great saltwater ponds dotting its terrain. It also boasts the magnificent beaches and idyllic panoramas that are part of the precious heritage of this French land.

The islands of St. Martin and St. Barts are swept by trade winds that blow from east to west over the

Typhoons, Cyclones and Hurricanes

Whether dealing with typhoons in Asia, cyclones in the southwestern part of the Indian Ocean or hurricanes in the Caribbean Sea, it is always a question of the same phenomenon: that is, a tropical (atmospheric) disturbance. Such disturbances are formed by the presence of large expanses of water at temperatures exceeding 26°C that span depths of several dozen metres. Hurricanes travel from east to west, accompanied by violent winds with velocities of over 120 km/h; they sometimes hit islands and cause considerable damage. This is what occurred in 1995, when Hurricane Luis, one of the most powerful hurricanes recorded in the 20th century, swept the coasts of St. Martin and St. Barts, destroying vegetation and devastating towns and hamlets alike. The inhabitants recovered quickly from this unbelievably intense natural disaster, and construction work was soon undertaken. Today, the traces of hurricane Luis have been more or less eradicated, and only the Dutch side of St. Martin (Sint Maarten) still bears a few scars.

Atlantic Ocean, carrying humid air with them. When this wind comes in contact with the islands' sheer mountainsides, the moisture-laden air condenses and turns into rain. Their eastern coasts, known as *côtes-au-vent* or windward coasts, are thus subjected to sudden downpours, allowing verdant vegetation to flourish here. Their western coasts, which face the Caribbean Sea, are sheltered from these winds by the very same mountains and are called *côtes-sous-le-vent*, or leeward coasts. Rarely subjected to sudden downpours, the vegetation growing on the west coasts is stunted and essentially composed of scrubs and cacti.

Flora and Fauna

Fauna

As in other parts of the Lesser Antilles that have never been connected to the American continent, wildlife is not very diverse on these volcanic islands sprung from the sea. In fact, the mammals that have proliferated here were all introduced by humans. Among these is the mongoose, introduced by European colonists in an effort to eliminate rats and venomous snakes (water moccasins) that destroyed crops. The mongoose also attacked various indigenous species, particularly ground-nesting birds that until then had no predators, and exterminated many of them.

Animal life is nevertheless abundant on the islands, and reptiles are particularly plentiful. Lizards, including the anole, ground anole, and Mabuya, are among the species that have evolved on these sun-drenched soils. These insectivores and omnivores can attain a maximum length of 30cm. **Iguanas**, which feed on plants and insects, are much larger and can grow to lengths of up to 1m. Although they can look intimidating, they are perfectly harmless.

Birds

Winged wildlife abounds on the islands, making a bird-watcher out of just about anyone who looks around. To help you identify these animals, we have included a description of the most common species below. With a bit of patience and a good pair of binoculars, you are sure to spot a few.

The **brown pelican** has greyish-brown plumage and is distinguished by its long neck and long grey beak with a large pouch. It is usually seen alone or in small groups, flying in single file. These birds, which can grow to up to 140cm, are commonly found near beaches.

Magnificent frigate bird

The wingspan of the jet-black **magnificent frigate bird** can reach up to 2.5m. The colour of the throat is the distinguishing mark between the sexes; the male's is red, the female's white. These birds can often be spotted gliding effortlessly over the waves in search of food.

The **kingfisher** is found in eastern North America and the Lesser Antilles. It is set apart by its blue plumage and white breast, but more specifically by its large head topped with a crested tuft. It can often be seen practically hovering in one spot before plunging into the waves in search of food.

Cattle egret

Herons are often found wading near mangrove swamps and fresh-water ponds. Among the different types is the **great heron**, which can grow to up to 132cm in height. It is identifiable by the large black feather extending from its white head down its neck. Its body is covered with grey and white plumage. You'll certainly spot the **cattle egret**, another bird in the same family commonly seen in the fields amongst the cattle. This bird is about 60cm tall, with white plumage and an orange tuft of feathers on its head. It arrived in the Caribbean during the 1950s; before that it was spotted only in Africa. It has adapted well and is found in large numbers throughout the Antilles. Finally, you'll probably hear the distinctive call of the little **green heron**. This bird grows to a height of 45cm and has greenish-grey feathers on its back and wings.

Visitors can catch a glimpse of the **black-necked stilt**, a wader measuring about 35cm in height, in the marshes and in the vicinity of the mangrove swamp. It is distinguished by its black back, wings, beak, the upper part of its head (including its eyes) which contrasts with its white underbelly and lower part of its head. Its legs are very thin and pink.

Black-necked stilt

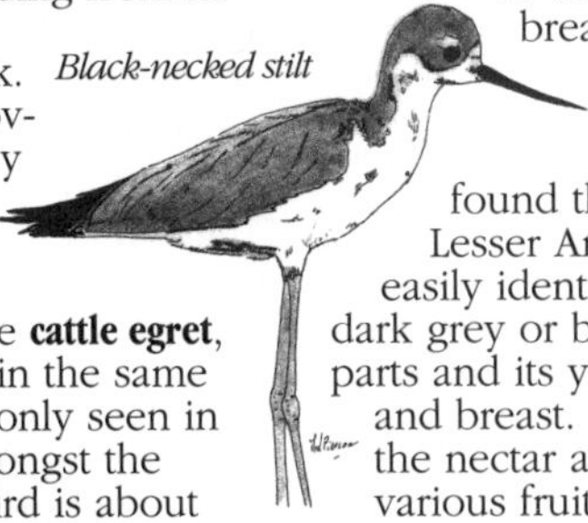

The **bananaquit**, also known as the yellow-breasted sunbird, is a small bird, about 10cm tall, found throughout the Lesser Antilles. It is easily identifiable by its dark grey or black upper parts and its yellow throat and breast. It feeds on the nectar and juice of various fruits, including bananas and papaya. This greedy little bird often sets down on a patio table for a bit of sugar.

The minuscule **humming-bird**, with its colourful plumage, feeds on insects and nectar and can be seen hovering about near flowering bushes and trees. Two types of hummingbird live on these islands. The **green-throated carib** can grow to up to 12cm and has black plumage with green iridescent feathers on its head and throat. The **antillean crested humming-bird**, the smallest hummingbird, weighing no more than 2g, has a blue and green crest.

Rainbow parrotfish

There are several types of turtledove on the islands, each about the size of a pigeon. The most common is the **zenaida dove**, with a brown back and a pinkish-beige breast, neck and head. It also has a blue spot on either side of its head. The **common turtledove** has greyish-brown plumage, with a black and white speckled neck.

The Ocean Depths

The shallow, perpetually warm waters (20°C) surrounding the islands provide a perfect environment for the growth of **coral**. Formed by a colony of minuscule organisms called coelenterate polyps growing on a polypary (calcareous skeleton), coral takes many different forms. These coral colonies have developed along the leeward coasts, protected from violent winds. The abundance of plankton around these formations attracts a wide variety of marine wildlife. Fish of all sizes also gravitate around the coral, including **tuna**, **kingfish**, more colourful fish like **parrotfish**, **boxfish**, **mullet**, **angelfish** and on rare occasions **sharks**. The coral is also home to numerous other animals, like **sponges** and **sea urchins**.

Flora

Though the windward coasts are covered in lush vegetation, most areas of these two Caribbean islands have only stunted flora because of the arid climate.

Palm Trees

Tall, stately palm trees dot the landscape of the Lesser Antilles. There are 2,779 varieties of this tree, which belongs to the monocotyledonous family. It grows in humid forests and deserts alike and can be found both in coastal regions and in the mountains. Except for palm creepers, all the species are similar. Their stalks, which have almost the same diameter at the base as at the top, are not trunks, but rather stipes that end in a fountain of leaves. The new leaves grow out of the middle of this "bouquet," while the old leaves fall off, revealing the stalk.

Some species of palms are put to multiple uses. For example, the stems of the royal palm, the red latan and the coconut palm are used in construction and their fruits (coconuts) are a popular food. Palm fronds are also used for roofing and to make hats.

Shrubs and cacti do their utmost to cling to the poor soil of steep hillsides and, in certain places, plants seem to grow out of the very rock.

Nevertheless, this scenery is teeming with multi-coloured flora. The incredibly vibrant flowers grow all year round, brightening the landscape with reds, pinks and brilliant yellows. Hibiscus, pink laurels, ballisiers, orchids and alpinias adorn gardens and parks. Trees and shrubs, such as bougainvilleas and flamboyants complete this luxuriant and utterly enchanting tableau with their flower-laden branches.

Unique flora grows in some areas along the coast, not to mention the marine vegetation that divers encounter in the deep.

The Coastal Landscapes

Magnificent stretches of white sandy beaches border much of the coast of St.

Barts and St. Martin; some, such as the glorious Orient Bay, are over 1km long. A particular type of vegetation flourishes along the edge of the beaches. It is essentially composed of sea-grape trees, easily recognizable by their clusters of large green fruit similar to grapes, as well as creeping lianas and palm trees. Another tree occasionally found near beaches is the dangerous manchineel, distinguished by its small, green, round leaves bisected by a yellow vein. These trees are generally marked by a red *X* or a warning sign, because they produce poisonous sap that can cause serious burns.

Mangrove tree

The Mangrove Swamp

This strange forest, growing in salt water and mud, consists mainly of mangroves (the most common being the red mangrove, recognizable by its aerial roots). Shrubs and plants also thrive in this swampland and, farther inland, the river mangrove develops in less briny waters. A vast quantity of organisms such as birds, crustaceans and, above all, a multitude of insects of all kinds, live in the heart of this impenetrable forest. This complex and fragile ecosystem plays an essential role for the islands' fauna as it provides both nourishment and shelter. In St. Martin, to the south of Orient Bay, the Baie de l'Embouchure offers a distant view of a mangrove swamp that was damaged by Hurricane Luis in 1995, and is slowly growing back.

History

Natives had settled in the Antilles long before Columbus ever discovered the New World. Much like other indigenous peoples, their ancestors came from northern Asia, crossing the Bering Strait toward the end of the ice age before inhabiting practically all of the Americas in successive migratory waves. Because of the Caribbean's geographical isolation, it was only later that these people ventured there.

Evidence suggests that the Ciboney, the first Arawak-speaking people to undertake the long voyage to the Caribbean Islands, arrived in St. Martin over 3,500 years ago. A thousand years later, a second wave of Arawak-speaking Andean people, the Huecoids, apparently came and settled here. The next group to reach the island was the Saladoids, also Arawak-speaking. This last group then migrated to the Dominican Republic, where it very likely encountered descendants of the Ciboneys. These two groups mingled (henceforth named "modified Saladoids") and returned to settle in St. Martin between AD 800 and 1200. A fishing people, they built their villages by the sea, from which they drew the greater part of their food. Relics found on the island of St. Martin bear witness to these ancient origins and migratory movements as well as to inhabitants' dexterity and skill.

For centuries, these Arawak-speaking peoples were the sole rulers of the islands, until another group, the Caribs (the fourth migratory wave from South America, from the region between the Orinoco and Amazon rivers), set their sights on this region. A fierce war was then waged against the Arawaks, who, ill-equipped to defend themselves, were unable to hold out against their foes and abandoned certain territories. Indeed, the Caribs came to control the whole of the Lesser Antilles. They came to St. Barts to fish for shellfish. It seems, however, that none went to St. Martin. Archaeological digs of Caribbean sites of the Lesser Antilles indicate that this group, known for its mastery in the making of weapons, particularly axes, did not inherit the artistic skills of its predecessors.

Discovery of the Antilles

On the morning of August 3, 1492, Christopher Columbus, financed by the Catholic kings of Spain and Aragon, headed a flotilla of three caravels, the *Santa Maria*, the *Pinta* and the

Niña, and undertook a voyage west in search of a new route to Asia. This two-month voyage across the Atlantic Ocean led him to the Caribbean archipelago, more specifically to one of the islands of the Bahamas known to natives as "Guanahani." Thus marking the official "discovery" of the Americas on October 12, 1492, Columbus and his men believed themselves to be just off the coast of Southeast Asia.

For a few weeks, Columbus and his crew explored Guanahani and the surrounding islands, establishing the first links with the indigenous peoples. He then continued on his way toward Cuba, skirting its coast. The Genoese sailor then proceeded toward the coast of another island, locally known as "Tohio," which he named "Isla Espagnola" (or Hispaniola). Following the coast and exploring part of this island, which he found magnificent, he soon envisaged the possibility of establishing a Spanish colony there. The shipwreck of the *Santa Maria* provided a perfect excuse to erect a fort here. A few weeks later, Columbus, fired with enthusiasm, returned to Spain, leaving 39 soldiers behind.

About 10 months elapsed before Columbus undertook a second voyage to the Americas. Upon his return to Hispaniola, he found no trace of the fort or the soldiers who had been slaughtered by the indigenous peoples. Might the soldiers have abused their hospitality? Whatever the case, punitive expeditions against the natives were undertaken as a result. Columbus, having returned with the necessary materials and men to found a Spanish city, did not allow himself to be discouraged by the incident, and proceeded to found the island's first city.

The natives of this island, the Arawaks, told Columbus of tribes on the other islands to the south, prompting him to continue exploring in that direction, thus discovering the chain of islands now known as the Lesser Antilles. The Genoese sailor remained undaunted by either the lack of potable water or the Caribs, the islands' inhabitants, who were prepared to fiercely defend their territory. He landed on several islands, including Dominica, and then continued on to Guadeloupe where he stayed for a time to replenish his stock of fresh water. He then took to the sea once again, heading north, where he came across St. Barts, which he named after his bother Bartolomé. On November 11, 1493, St. Martin's Day, he happened upon yet another small island, which he named in honour of the saint.

No doubt due to the lack of men needed to populate all these new lands and because of the Caribs who inhabited them, the Spanish decided not to colonize the Lesser Antilles but, rather, to concentrate their efforts on the Greater Antilles. Many years passed before a colony was established in the Lesser Antilles. In the meantime, the islands served mainly as stopovers for the privateers and sailors navigating these waters.

The Birth of the West Indian Colonies

Only the Spanish and Portuguese succeeded in colonizing the New World in the 15th century. Their boats arrived in Europe full of treasures taken from indigenous peoples and quickly became targeted by smugglers and pirates who criss-crossed the seas, looting them for the spoils. These treasures showed the rest of Europe the riches to be reaped by claiming these lands to the west.

Around 1623, the French privateer D'Esnambuc sailed for the Lesser Antilles. After having attacked the Spanish at sea, he sought refuge on Saint-Christophe to repair his vessel. The English navigator Warner was already on the island, but the two managed to divide the territory among themselves. Upon his return to France, d'Esnambuc had these boundaries ratified, and founded the Compagnie Saint-Christophe under the patronage of Richelieu, who held a high-ranking administrative position and was in charge of the exploitation of new territories, in addition to having trading rights.

The Partition of St. Martin

Apparently, the partition of St. Martin was brought about very simply: two men were dispatched from opposite sides of the island and the point at which they met determined the dividing line. France thus acquired three fifths of the island, while the Netherlands procured a smaller portion, but one that had greater natural resources.

During the following years, France pursued the colonization of the Lesser Antilles much more aggressively.

The Compagnie des Îles d'Amérique replaced the Compagnie Saint-Christophe in 1635, with a mandate to conquer the territories situated between 10° and 30° latitude north.

France, however, was not the only European power with an eye on the Antilles; the Dutch were also attempting to colonize the islands. In 1621, the first Dutch company was created. Known as the West Indies Company (Colbert created another company with the same name in later years), it undertook the conquest of several islands in the Lesser Antilles, including Saint-Martin, Aruba, Bonaire and Curaçao. In 1638, the Dutch built a fort on St. Martin, having found significant salt deposits on the island.

St. Martin was quickly reconquered by the Spanish, who wanted to maintain control of the island, since it was a stopping point for many ships. In 1638, 9,000 Spanish soldiers were sent to supervise the territory. This manoeuvre quickly proved less strategic than the Spanish had thought; realizing the futility of their actions, they abandoned the island less than 10 years later, leaving the field wide open for other colonists.

Colonization

Little by little, the conquest of the Lesser Antilles was undertaken by the French. Two men, Liénart de l'Olive and du Plessis, convinced the Compagnie des Îles d'Amérique of the necessity of colonizing Guadeloupe. Accompanied by 500 men and a few representatives of the church (including Père Duterte), they arrived on June 28, 1635. Acclimatization proved difficult, however, and the men suffered from a lack of supplies, epidemics and famine. Establishing this new colony also entailed waging a brutal war against the Caribs, which further hampered colonists' efforts.

The first attempt at colonizing Guadeloupe changed nothing with respect to the administration of the territories, and the seat of the French colonies remained in Saint-Christophe (present-day Saint Kitts). In 1638, following the death of Liénart de l'Olive and du Plessis, Poincy de Lonvilliers, then governor, devised a plan to transfer the capital (Saint-Christophe) to Guadeloupe. This move would have favoured the latter's development had it not been thwarted by conflicts between the governor's personal ambitions, the interests of the *compagnie* executives back in France and those of the other representatives in the islands.

This period of instability did nothing to reassure the colonists of Saint-Christ-ophe, some of whom, considering the situation precarious, decided to try their luck elsewhere. Thus, four French colonists left Saint-Christophe in 1648, disembarking on St. Martin with the aim of settling there. They were not alone in coveting the island abandoned by Spanish troops, however, for the Dutch government, having the same designs, had sent Martin Thomas to take possession of the territory. Rather than engaging in ruthless warfare, these new arrivals opted for an equitable partition of the island.

That same year, convinced of the importance of colonizing each of the islets in the Lesser Antilles, Poincy de Lonvilliers sent Sieur Jacques de Gente along with about 50 colonists to populate St. Barts. Devoid of lakes and rivers and possessing poor soil, the island had everything to discourage these new arrivals who, left to themselves, had to persevere in order to survive.

Agreements aimed at ending the war between the French and the Caribs were reached at this time (1641), and the colony experienced a period of peace. The respite was welcomed by the colonists, who needed time to get settled, and by the Compagnie des Îles d'Amérique, which found the colonies expensive. Famine, war against the Caribs, bad weather and countless other problems eventually forced the company to sell its possessions. It sold Saint-Christophe in 1647 and then gave up its other islands. Along with St. Barts, Saint-Martin became a possession of the Order of Malta in 1651.

This change of administration resulted in little change for the colonists; they still had to endure difficult living conditions and the hostility of the native population, which was fiercely set on preserving its land. Cohabitation between these two communities was difficult, and the slightest indiscretion became a source of violent conflict. Indeed, the inhabitants of St. Barts paid the price in 1656, when the Caribs, bent on revenge against the colonists, undertook various reprisals against the French colonies and, upon reaching the shores of St. Barts, slaughtered all its inhabitants. Its colony annihilated, the island was abandoned for almost four years. Despite this blow, the will to colonize it remained steadfast and the island was repopulated in 1659 when a second group of Bretons, Normans and Poitevins came to settle there.

The Order of Malta

Originally called the "Knights of the Hospital of Saint John of Jerusalem," the Order of Malta was founded during the Crusades to protect and care for pilgrims on their way to Palestine (AD 1113). Despite their active role in the Crusades, the knights had to withdraw when the Holy Land was lost. The Order thus relocated to Cyprus. It wasn't until 1530, when Charles V gave up the island of Malta, that these knights took the name "the knights of Malta." By the time it purchased certain Caribbean possessions, the Order of Malta was rich and powerful.

These Caribbean colonies developed gradually, despite early obstacles and a precarious economic situation. In order to encourage their growth, Colbert, who began attending to the French kingdom's affairs in 1661, decided to create a powerful company backed by the king, which would manage all the colonies. The Compagnie des Indes Occidentales was thus founded on May 13, 1664. On July 10th of the same year, Guadeloupe, Martinique and Saint-Christophe were acquired by the company; the following year, Saint-Martin (the French side) and St. Barts were purchased as well. Colbert's intentions were not fully realized, however, because, although the company had a monopoly on trade between these islands and France's colonies in the Americas, it was deemed too unprofitable and was forced to cease operations. In 1674, the company's possessions were transferred to the French Crown.

Through these difficult first 50 years of colonization, the French and the Dutch succeeded in establishing themselves in the Antilles. This, however, had harsh consequences for the Carib and Arawak populations, which were ruthlessly attacked by the colonists seeking to appropriate their lands. Not numerous enough to resist these foreign offensives, the Caribs were decimated and the

Arawaks exterminated. In 1660, the last Caribs were expelled from all French possessions and relocated in Dominica and St. Vincent. Their descendants still live in Dominica today.

The Emergence of a Distinct Caribbean Economy

While the governors tried to get richer, newly arrived colonists in the Antilles had to settle in and develop greater self-sufficiency, since it was always difficult to secure supplies from France. Crops like yams, peas, indigo, tobacco and cotton provided food and modest revenue from trade with France.

The introduction of sugar cane to the Antilles (around 1650 in St. Martin) shook up the island's economy, as sugar was becoming more and more prized on the European market, making for handsome returns for the colonists. A problem quickly presented itself to farmers, though: harvesting sugar cane requires a large workforce. There were not enough inhabitants on the island at the time, so efforts were made to increase the population. At first, the leaders of the colonies tried to attract French farmers by setting up a recruitment program. The program was very demanding for future colonists, who had to sign up for 36 months. During this time they could not enter into any contracts and essentially signed over their freedom and their labour to their master. In exchange they received a piece of land or sum of money at the end of the contract. The horrible living conditions of the recruits (poor treatment, insufficient food, sickness) in most cases led to death or abandonment before the end of the term. It is therefore no surprise that, as of 1668, the recruitment of French workers was practically non-existent. Another solution would have to be found to the workforce problem.

Slavery was quickly presented as the only inexpensive solution, and colonists set their sights on the coast of western Africa, from where countless Africans were taken by force and shipped off to the Caribbean. These men and women, sent by sea in the most horrible and inhumane conditions (many of them died en route), arrived in St. Martin. Sold to land-owning colonists, they soon formed a large workforce.

The introduction of slavery thus enabled the people of St. Martin to undertake the cultivation of sugar cane and, though the arid land received little rain and the

The Code Noir

In 1685, the French government passed an edict called the Code Noir. This law established the fates of slaves, whose number exceeded that of Whites and free *colons*. In particular, it stated that slaves had to be part of someone's chattels, and the owner had complete control over them. It also laid down the extent of the master's repressive powers. The Code Noir did, however, recognize some rights of slaves, such as the master's obligation to feed and clothe them. It also defined working conditions. Finally, it set out the status of free people of colour, a status which was neither that of Whites nor of slaves. To a certain extent, it institutionalized the social segregation of Blacks, people of colour and Whites.

crop yield proved somewhat meagre, the inhabitants prospered. This growth, however, was restricted by limits imposed by the mother countries, who did not want the islands' commodities to compete with the products of French and Dutch farmers.

With the passing years, the population of black slaves grew considerably, and soon made up the majority of the sugar islands' (St. Martin, Guadeloupe, Martinique) inhabitants, resulting in major social tensions. In an effort to counter the "dangers" of a black-slave majority, harsh policies were adopted to control the slaves. This, of course, did little to appease the people's anger, as the number of uprisings in this period demonstrate.

St. Barts: An Exceptional History

Much like Guadeloupe and Martinique, St. Martin succeeded in developing an economy based on the sale of sugar cane. Conversely, St. Barts, whose soil proved too poor to support this type of cultivation, was deprived of the prosperity enjoyed by its sister islands; its inhabitants had to content themselves with farm ing, which just barely provided for their needs. Their lives were made all the more difficult by the frequent and devastating foreign incursions besetting their land, which was practically indefensible and consequently devoid of garrisons. Enemy troops were not alone in coveting this islet: early on, privateers and pirates saw it as an ideal refuge. Though somewhat questionable, these new arrivals were nevertheless able to trade with the inhabitants, which led to their cohabitation: the privateers benefited from Anse du Carénage (as Gustavia was once known; carénage is the French word for careenage, a place to careen, or tip, a boat in order to clean its hull), while the residents of St. Barts withdrew into the island's interior.

This strange proximity was not, however, without consequences for the small colony, for several denizens of St. Barts, exasperated by foreign attacks, chose to become pirates as well and pillaged foreign vessels skirting the coast. This new activity around the coast of St. Barts enabled the small colony to grow, and a village soon grew around Carénage.

This modest boom only lasted about 20 years, however, for the English, exasperated by the frequent assaults, attacked the island in 1744, capturing the privateers and replacing them with their own, who pillaged and slaughtered the remaining inhabitants. Despite the violence of this attack, it did not end the French colonization of St. Barts, because the British governor, condemning the excesses of his troops, would later allow the survivors who had managed to find refuge on Saint-Christophe to return to their island.

During the 18th century, devastating foreign incursions were numerous and, much like France's other possessions (including Saint-Martin), their island was brought under British control on more than one occasion. At the end of the Seven Years War (Treaty of Paris, 1763), France lost out to the British and was forced to surrender some of its colonies. In order to keep its profitable sugar-producing colonies of Martinique, Guadeloupe and Saint-Martin (St. Barts was also restored to France due to an oversight in the treaty), France abandoned its possessions in North America.

St. Martin and the Slow March to Emancipation

The end of the 18th century was a particularly turbulent time for St. Martin, Guadeloupe and Martinique, as much due to instability caused by foreign incursions as to racial tensions that were reaching their peak. Such was the explosive context in the Antilles when the French Revolution occurred in 1789, leading to the abolition of the monarchy. This considerable upheaval that struck France had its consequences in the islands, where deep dissension was brewing. Certain large property owners saw an opportunity to end the trade restrictions imposed by the French government, thus giving the colony greater autonomy. At the same time, anti-slavery movements came up against owners who favoured a hard line on slaves. Finally, the small property-owners anticipated playing a more important political role, thereby getting out from under the yoke of the large property-owners and the aristocrats. All of this dissent exploded in the wake of the events of 1789.

In February 1794, English troops arrived in Martinique, Guadeloupe and Saint-Martin and took advantage of this internal disorder to overthrow the existing administration. Victor Hugues was sent to Guadeloupe to counter the English invasion. Along with 14 frigates and 18 warships full of men, Hugues was backed by all the black slaves, to whom he had promised freedom. Hugues arrived in Guadeloupe in June, and by December had succeeded in pushing back the English. Saint-Martin was liberated in 1796, and Hugues took this opportunity to annex the Dutch part of the island, which France would keep until 1801.

During this period, the slaves were set free. Their liberty did not last long, however, as bit by bit the governors that followed Hugues revoked the rights accorded the blacks. Under

Napoleon's government, slavery was actually reinstated.

The island of St. Martin fell once more to English conquerors, who occupied the island in 1808 and ruled it until 1815. The signing of the Treaty of Vienna put an end to Caribbean rivalries between these two European powers. Peace was thus restored to the small colony, which progressively changed as anti-slavery movements mobilized; slavery was abolished in British colonies as of 1833. The abolition of slavery in the French colonies was not instituted until 1848, however, when an official decree was initiated by Victor Schœlcher. Slaves inhabiting the Dutch part of St. Martin were not freed until 1863.

The abolition of slavery had major consequences for residents of St. Martin. Living conditions for recently freed blacks remained precarious, and the whole economy had to be restructured in order to provide wages for this previously unpaid workforce. This restructuring raised the production costs of sugar, thus causing a major crisis in the industry. In order to remedy this delicate economic situation, large sugar companies were formed through small mergers, thereby offering jobs to the local workforce. As a result, many of the smaller farmers were forced into bankruptcy. Sugar cane production nevertheless remained difficult in St. Martin due to lack of rain and water, and local inhabitants gradually gave up. The island's salt reserves and status as a free port, acquired in 1850, led sailors to use its port installations and brought in the bulk of its meagre revenue.

St. Barts and Nearly a Century of Swedish Colonization

The few hundred years leading to the liberation of slaves in Caribbean colonies were quite different in St. Barts, where there were virtually no slaves. This period was particularly distinct because the island was sold to Sweden in 1785 by King Louis XVI, who deemed it more profitable to have the right to trade with Sweden (he acquired a warehouse in Gothenburg in exchange) than to keep this arid land.

This exchange proved beneficial for the residents of St. Barts, at least as far as their economy was concerned, for a number of favourable policies were adopted on their behalf. Carénage, the island's port, was renamed “Gustavia” (in honour of the Swedish

Important Dates in History

1493: Christopher Columbus discovers the Lesser Antilles, including Guadeloupe, Marie-Galante, La Désirade, Les Saintes, St. Barts and St. Martin. At the time, the islands are inhabited by Caribs.

1635: The Compagnie de Saint-Christophe gets French colonization underway in the Caribbean.

1638: Spanish troops entrench themselves on St. Martin.

1648: St. Martin is colonized by the French and the Dutch, who share the territory. A first group of colonists settles on St. Barts, but is massacred by the Caribs.

1651: St. Martin becomes a possession of the Order of Malta.

1659: A second contingent of Bretons, Normans and Poitevins establishes itself on St. Barts.

1660: The Carib people are decimated or deported from the French territories to Dominica.

1664: The Order of Malta sells its Caribbean possessions to the Compagnie des Indes Occidentales, founded by Colbert.

1674: Following the bankruptcy of the Compagnie des Indes Occidentales, its Caribbean possessions become attached to the French Crown.

Late 17th century: African people are brought to the islands as slaves.

1785: St. Barts is sold to the Swedish for the French right to trade in Swedish territory.

1789: Revolution rocks France with important consequences for the administration of the colonies. The slaves are freed.

1802: Napoleon's troops land on St. Martin and re-establish slavery.

1848: Slavery is definitively abolished in the French Antilles.

1877: Sweden cedes St. Barts back to France.

1946: Guadeloupe and Martinique become overseas French departments. St. Barts and St. Martin are administratively tied to Guadeloupe.

1995: Hurricane Luis hits St. Martin and St. Barts.

king, Gustave III) in 1785 by governor Salomon Mauritz von Rayalin, and became a free port. A few years later, when the inhabitants' poverty came to his attention, Gustave III granted them tax exemptions. The period between 1795 and 1820 was particularly prosperous thanks to greatly increased activity at the port. Despite this new-found affluence, however, inhabitants of St. Barts who were of French origin had trouble accepting this new authority. They kept to themselves, rarely mingled with Swedes and refused to submit to the Swedish governors.

This wealth, however, was only to last about 20 years; after 1820, St. Barts' port was abandoned in favour of other islands, precipitating yet another economic decline. Moreover, the island was rocked by a series of natural disasters, making it a far less attractive possession. Furthermore, the inhabitants were already so poor that, in the days following the abolition of slavery, no one could afford to pay their workers, and the few freed slaves, having no other resources, had no choice but to seek exile.

During the 19th century, the situation on the island was such that the Swedish government saw no advantage in keeping it and sought to relinquish it. St. Barts was thus ceded back to France on August 10, 1877, in exchange for a sum of 400,000 francs and the obligation to leave its residents exempt from taxes, a situation that has remained unchanged to this day. This treaty was ratified by the great majority of the population, which became French once again. The island was administratively tied to Guadeloupe, which also comprised the French portion of St. Martin.

The Late 19th and the 20th Centuries

In 1877, St. Barts was grafted to the other French Caribbean colonies, which had just survived years that were difficult at best; some had seen their economies completely collapse. In St. Martin the gains drawn from the sugar trade had disappeared and the island's sole source of revenue was its port. The people of St. Barts survived on the modest returns from agriculture and fishing.

The 20th century brought its own lot of hardships. The outbreak of the First World War in 1914 had major repercussions for St. Martin and St. Barts, which sent their own contingents of soldiers to support France's efforts. The Netherlands remained neutral throughout this conflict.

Between the two wars, the two tax-exempt islands' economies prospered. Commerce and trade in general, but especially of tobacco and liquor, were favoured. In fact, the islands were a central part of the illegal liquor trade during the years of prohibition in the United States.

Before long, another catastrophe rocked Europe: the Second World War, which began on September 3, 1939. Less than a year later the Netherlands (May 10, 1940) and France (June 16, 1940) fell to the Germans, but the administrative consequences were negligible for the islands. Both countries were liberated in 1945.

On March 19, 1946, an important law concerning Guadeloupe, its dependencies and Martinique was adopted, when these colonies were established as overseas French departments or *départements français d'outre-mer.* The French side of Saint-Martin became part of the department of Guadeloupe. Both islands experienced significant economic development, thanks to the growth of the tourism industry, which flourished from the beginning of the 1980s.

Economy

The arid soil of St. Martin, and particularly that of St. Barts, prevented the two little islands from ever experiencing the boom brought on by the sugar industry. In St. Martin, the cultivation of sugar cane was possible, but never productive enough, and had to be abandoned in the 19th century when a crisis in the sugar industry compromised any prospect of profit. The inhabitants of St. Barts, meanwhile, were obliged to fall back on the cultivation of a handful of crops like cotton and then pineapple in the 19th century, which just barely allowed the colonists to remain self-sufficient. Over the years, other industries, such as fishing, salt mining (from rich deposits on the Dutch side of St. Martin) and port infrastructures enabled the inhabitants to improve their living conditions, though they never ensured their prosperity.

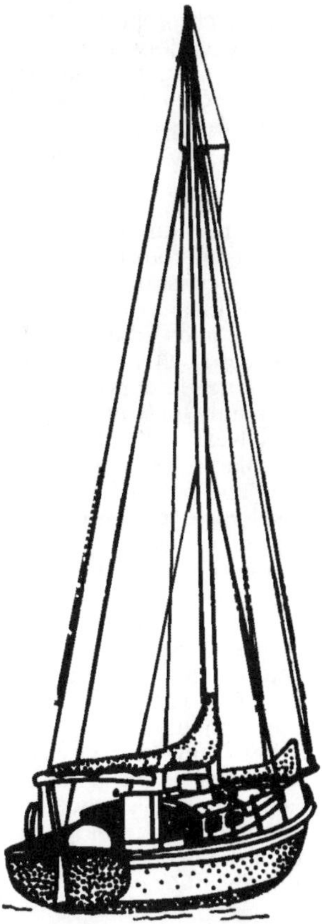

Nevertheless, these little islands in the north of the archipelago, administratively tied to Guadeloupe, which itself still had a ways to go in structuring its own economy, were too often neglected and could never count on its help. The Dutch part of the island, Sint Maarten, experienced similar economic difficulties due to its distance from other Dutch properties. On several occasions, the Dutch inhabitants preferred seeking exile further south, on the islands of Aruba and Curaçao, which had more to offer.

The 20th century brought more prosperous times. First, the construction of the Princess Juliana airport (Sint Maarten) allowed the island to develop better relations with its neighbours, most importantly the United States. Next, the Dutch part of St. Martin became a tax haven and profited from considerable foreign investment, which led to the expansion of its tourist industry. Sint Maarten's tourist industry was so huge that the Dutch territory welcomed the most tourists (500,000 in 1995) of all the Lesser Antilles. In its shadow, Saint-Martin, which thrived because of its status as a free port, also saw its tourist industry develop into one of the mainstays of its economy.

St. Barts, whose residents have been free from taxation since 1785 (a measure implemented in response to their extreme poverty), also presents undeniable advantages attractive to investors. At the beginning of the 1980s, it also experienced important growth in the tourism industry. Given the small size of its territory, St. Barts has always successfully catered to wealthy visitors.

Both islands live with and by the comings and goings of tourists, attracted by their sunny beaches and natural setting. Though some have profited from the tourism boom, there is still a large disparity on St. Martin between the rich French, Dutch and foreign minority and the working-class majority, who live in very modest conditions.

Politics

St. Martin and St. Barts

Since the law of March 19, 1946 came into effect, Guadeloupe has been a *département français d'outre-mer* or DOM, and Saint-Martin and St. Barts have been designated *cantons*. In 1963, St. Martin was elevated to a *sous-préfecture* (the *sous-préfecture* of the northern islands is made up of Saint-Martin, Tintamarre and St. Barts). In accordance with the constitution, they have two political assemblies: the Conseil Régional, based on a system of proportional representation, and the Conseil Général, elected by a two-round majority vote. The Conseil Régional handles economic and regional development and workforce training, while the Conseil Général looks after social concerns. These two assemblies have the power to legislate within their respective domains and determine appropriate budgets as well. Besides the Conseil Régional and the Conseil Général, the department has a Comité Économique et Social and a Comité de la Culture et de l'Evironnement. Four deputies represent the department in the French Assemblée Nationale, and two senators in the Sénat.

Citizens of the French section of St. Martin, as well as those of St. Barts, enjoy the same social programs as citizens of France, including old age pensions, family allowances, unemployment insurance and health insurance. However, these programs are not always administered in the same way here as they are in continental Europe.

During the last few decades, politics in the French overseas department of Guadeloupe, of which St. Martin and St. Barts are a part, have been particularly marked by demands for autonomy from the mother country. However, since the social structure of St. Martin and St. Barts is very different from that of Guadeloupe itself, these two islands' populations have never been in favour of separation, at the very most wanting greater economic independence.

Sint Maarten

Sint Maarten is part of the kingdom of the Netherlands, and its inhabitants are subjected to a very different political system than that of the French side of the island, since the Netherlands granted it full autonomy in internal affairs. The kingdom encompasses three countries: the Netherlands proper, and the overseas departments of Aruba and the Netherlands Antilles; the latter includes Bonaire, Curaçao, Saba, Sint Eustatius and Sint Maarten. Though they remain dependencies, each of these countries has its own parliament elected by popular vote, as well as a cabinet and a prime minister. The government has the power to legislate and is responsible for local affairs, including social and medical services, education, economic development, road maintenance, tourism promotion and sports. It also oversees water and electricity distribution as well as port and airport installations, which are run by state-sponsored companies. Foreign affairs, defence and judicial affairs remain the responsibility of the kingdom of the Netherlands.

Thus, unlike the French part of the island, Sint Maarten creates its own policy on issues related to its development, most notably its social programs. This greater level of autonomy means that Sint Maarten's social programs are not necessarily the same as those of the Netherlands.

Population

The flourishing economy, the sun and St. Martin's status as a free port have attracted many immigrants to the island. In fact, the population is growing by leaps and bounds, increasing from 10,000 (in either part of the island) at the beginning of the 1980s to nearly 30,000 in the French part and more than 39,000 in Dutch part in about 15 years. To these official numbers must be added between 5,000 and 30,000 illegal residents (the coasts are hard to supervise) living on the island. Such foreigners have swelled the ranks of the rich immigrants who make up only a tiny portion of newcomers to the island. People have come from many different countries; it is said that 70 nationalities are represented on the island. In fact, there are so many immigrants, that Creoles no longer form a majority on this little island.

It is a completely different story in St. Barts, where 95% of its approximately 5,000 inhabitants are white, many of them of Norman, Breton or Poitevin descent. Long isolated, this tiny society has a reputation for being very closed and not very welcoming to new arrivals. Indeed, it does everything possible to counter the arrival of illegal foreign workers on its territory.

Culture

St. Martin

The increasing influence of the United States, which has characterized the second half of the 20th century, has led to the Americanization of local culture here as in other places. St. Martin has had more contact with this giant than its sister island,

The Architecture of the Creole Cottage

Though the wooden cottages scattered throughout St. Martin and St. Barts may appear quite fragile, they were designed to withstand the capricious climate of the Caribbean islands. Comprising two to three rooms and rarely measuring more than 21m^2, the wooden Creole cottage is the most common local dwelling. These houses were built on sites carefully chosen to ensure their solidity. Before assembling the framework, a stone foundation was laid out to protect the wood from dampness. Four pillars were then erected (at each corner of the house), after which the frame was raised. Overlaid with wooden planks, some were sided with wooden shingles (called *essentes* here), making them more watertight. The roof was made of dried grasses, palm fronds, or shingles, according to the occupant's means. All the wooden pieces could be easily dismantled, making them easier to move, because though most people owned their cottages, they often did not own the land on which they were built.

Today, wooden cottages, whose architecture is largely inspired by the wooden Creole cottage, are still built but are painted with lovely colours and often embellished with lacy wood trim, balconies and shutters. Indeed, all these ornaments make these living quarters quite pleasant.

In St. Barts, *cabrettes*, a type of dwelling particular to its windward side, are designed to withstand the occasionally violent winds blowing in from the ocean. The foundations of these very low cottages are almost the same as those of the Creole cottages, but the walls around the framework have been reinforced by large stones, bound together with a mix of earth and water and coated with a roughcast of lime. None of the cottages' entrances face the wind, and their few windows and doors are protected by large wooden shutters. The cottages thereby offer their occupants suitable protection from the elements.

Guadeloupe. Moreover, the mother tongue of a good many locals is no longer French or Dutch, but English. The massive influx of immigrants and tourists has also played a great part in shaping a very different society on this Caribbean island. It is therefore no longer a predominantly Creole culture as was once the case, but rather a multiethnic one.

St. Barts

Because of its history and demographics, St. Barts stands apart from the other French Caribbean islands. The cultural mingling so characteristic of the Antilles never occurred here; its inhabitants are primarily of French extraction. Long isolated from the metropolis just as they were from other Caribbean islands, and having inherited barren soil, the inhabitants of St. Barts have persevered throughout the centuries and resisted foreign occupations while preserving the essentials of their French heritage. Their language is peppered with certain archaisms and terms borrowed from the vocabulary of sailors, so much a legacy of their Breton, Norman, Vendée or Poitevin ancestors. Surprisingly, the population fought to stay on the island for decades, despite the difficulties of living here. Traditionally, its men have sought work on other islands, but have always retained St. Barts as their home and kept their families here. Is it any wonder, then, that this small community has the reputation for being closed and exclusive to this day?

St. Martin, Saint-Martin or Sint Maarten? St. Barts, Saint-Barth or Saint-Barthélemy?

The use of the hyphen in "Saint-Martin" reflects the French style of hyphenation and in this guide refers to the French side of the island. "Sint Maarten" is the Dutch name for the island and refers to the Dutch side of the island. We have chosen to refer to the island as a whole as "St. Martin."

"St. Barts" is the English name of the French island of Saint-Barthélemy and the one used in this guide. In French, it is often abbreviated to Saint-Barth.

Practical Information

Travelling throughout St. Martin and St. Barts is easy, whether you go by yourself or with an organized tour.

In Sint Maarten (the Dutch side) the locals speak English, while French is the official language in Saint-Martin and St. Barts. Most people working in stores, restaurants and hotels understand and speak at least a bit of English. However, there is a French-English glossary at the end of this guide, should you run into any problems. Being able to communicate is not all there is to preparing for a trip. This chapter will familiarize you with some of the local customs so that you can make the most of your vacation time.

The area code for Dutch Sint Maarten is **599**. Note that following changes to the telephone system, all telephone numbers begin with **54**, which is followed by five digits. In the French territory (Saint-Martin and St. Barts), all numbers begin with **05.90**, which you must dial whether you are calling from within or beyond this area.

Entrance Formalities

Canadians, Americans and citizens of countries belonging to the EU do not need a visa for stays of less than three months. They do, however, need a passport that is valid for the length of their stay, and a return or ongoing ticket. Other travellers are admitted for three weeks.

French visitors only need their national identity card, or *carte nationale d'identité*, to enter the country.

These regulations could change at any time, and travellers are advised to check with a French or Dutch embassy or consulate prior to your departure.

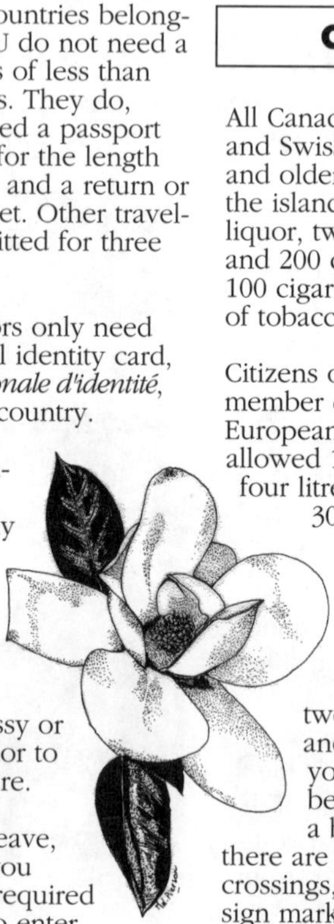

Before you leave, ensure that you have all the required documents to enter and leave the islands. Keep these documents in a safe place during your trip. It is also a good idea to keep a photocopy of the pertinent pages of your passport, as well as your passport number and its expiry date in a separate safe place, in case the original is lost. If this should happen, contact your country's embassy or consulate in order to have it replaced.

Customs

All Canadian, American, and Swiss visitors aged 17 and older are allowed onto the islands with one litre of liquor, two litres of wine and 200 cigarettes, 100 cigarillos or 250 grams of tobacco.

Citizens of legal age from member countries of the European Community are allowed 1.5 litres of spirits, four litres of wine and 300 cigarettes, 150 cigarillos or 400 grams of tobacco.

When travelling on St. Martin between the French and Dutch territories, you will not always be aware of crossing a border because there are no official border crossings, only a simple sign marking the border. Therefore, you need not worry about customs or papers. If you decide to fly from St. Martin to St. Barts, you will leave from the airport in Sint Maarten, which means you wil be taking an international flight and thus will need your passport (unless you are French).

Departure Tax

The islands of St. Martin and St. Barts are tax-free, though there is one exception for travellers. When leaving the island of St. Martin through Princess Juliana Airport, all travellers aged two years of age and older must pay a departure tax of US$20 (160 F).

The departure tax for St. Barts is included in the price of your airline ticket.

Foreign Consulates and Embassies

Consulates can be an invaluable source of help to visitors who find themselves in trouble. For example, consulates can provide names of doctors or lawyers in the case of death or serious injury. However, only urgent cases are handled. It should be noted that the cost of these services is not absorbed by the consulates.

There are no embassies on St. Martin or St. Barts; the closest consular offices to these two islands are listed below.

CANADA
72 South Quay, Box 1246, Port-of-Spain, Trinidad and Tobago
☎ ***(809) 623-7254 or 625-6734***
⇄ ***(809) 624-4016***

GERMANY
7-9 Marli St., Newtown
P.O. Box 828, Port-of-Spain, Trinidad and Tobego
☎ ***(868) 628-1630***
⇄ ***(868) 628-5278***

GREAT BRITAIN
Lower Collymore Rock, Box 676, Bridgetown City, Barbados
☎ ***(246) 430 7836***
⇄ ***(246)430 7860***
www.britishhc.org

NETHERLANDS
PO Box 870
Life of Barbados Building, 3rd floor
69-71 Edward St.
Port of Spain, Trinidad and Tobago
☎ ***(868) 625-1210 /1722 /2532***
⇄ ***(868) 625-1704***

DENMARK
20-22 Tragarete Rd,
Trinidad and Tobago
☎ ***(868) 625-1156***
⇄ ***(868) 623-8693***

SWEDEN
26 Windsor Rd.
Goodwood Park
Pt. Cumana
Port of Spain, Trinidad and Tobago
☎ ***(868) 632-0261***
⇄ ***(868) 633-9237***

Practical Information

United States Embassy
P.O. Box 302, Bridgetown,
Barbados, W.I.
☎ ***(246) 436-4950***

Embassies, Consulates and French Tourism Offices (Saint-Martin) Abroad

Canada
Maison de la France
1981, Avenue McGill College
Montréal, Québec, H3A 2W9
☎ ***(514) 288-4264***
⇄ ***(514) 845-4868***

Germany
Frankreich-Information
Postfach 100128
60001 FRANKFURT/MAIN
☎ ***(49) 0190 57 00 25***
⇄ ***(49) 0190 59 90 61***

Great Britain
Maison de la France
178 Piccadilly, London W1J 9AL
☎ ***(44) 09068 244 123***
⇄ ***(44) 207 493 65 94***

Netherlands
Maison de la France
Prinsengracht 670,
1017 KX Amsterdam
☎ ***(31) 20.627.33.18***
⇄ ***(31) 20.620.33.39***

United States
Maison de la France
444 Madison Ave., 16th Floor
New York, NY 10022-6903
☎ ***(212) 838-7800***
⇄ ***(212) 838-7855***

Maison de la France
676 North Michigan Ave., Suite 3360,
Chicago, Illinois 60611-2819
☎ ***(312) 751-7800***
⇄ ***(312) 337-6339***

Maison de la France
9454 Wilshire Blvd., Suite 715, Beverly
Hills, California 90212-2967
☎ ***(310) 271-6665***
⇄ ***(310) 276-2835***

Sweden
Maison de la France
Franska Turistbyråån
Norrmalmstorg 1A
11146 Stockholm
☎ ***46 8 566 112 00***
⇄ ***46 8 566 112 12***

DENMARK
Maison de la France
Det Franske Turistkontor
Ny ØØstergade 3,3
DK-1101 Copenhagen K
☎ ***45 33 11 49 12***
⇄ ***45 33 14 20 48***

Embassies, Consulates and Dutch Tourism Offices (Sint Maartin) Abroad

Canada
Sint Maarten Tourist Office
703 Evans Ave., Suite 106
Toronto ON M9C 5E9
☎ ***(416) 622-1680***
⇄ ***(416) 622-3438***

UNITED STATES
Sint Maarten Tourist Office
c/o Roy and P. Moss, 675 Third Ave., Suite 2300, New York, NY 10017
☎ ***(212) 953-2084 or 800-786-2278***

GERMANY
Netherlands Board of Tourism
Friesenplatz 1
PO Box 270580
50511 Cologne 1
☎ ***49 221 92571727***
⇄ ***49 221 92571737***
http://www.niederlande.de/

GREAT BRITIAN
Netherlands Board of Tourism
PO Box 523
London SW1E 6NT
☎ ***0906 871 7777***
⇄ ***44 (0)20 7828 7941***

SWEDEN
Royal Netherlands Embassy
Göötgatan 16 A
PO Box 15048
104 65 Stockholm
☎ ***46 8 556 933 00***
⇄ ***46 8 556 933 11***

DENMARK
Royal Netherlands Embassy
Toldbodgade 33
1253 Copenhagen K.
Denmark
☎ ***45 33 70 72 00***
⇄ ***45 33 14 03 50***

Tourist Information on St. Martin

Saint-Martin

Office du Tourisme de Saint-Martin
Route de Sandy Ground
Marigot
☎ ***05.90.87.57.21***
⇄ ***05.90.87.56.43***
www.st-martin.org
www.frenchcaribbean.com

Sint-Maarten

St. Maarten Tourist Bureau
Imperial Building, 23 Walter Nisbeth Rd., Philipsburg
☎ ***(599) 542-2337***
⇄ ***(599) 542-2734***
www.st-maarten.com

Tourist Information on St. Barts

Quai du Général De Gaulle
Gustavia, 97095
☎ ***05.90.27.87.27***
⇄ ***05.90.27.74.47***
www.saint-barths.com

Getting to St. Martin

The island of St. Martin has two international airports; on the French side is L'Espérance Airport (near Grand Case), which is only equipped to receive small planes, although most travellers arrive at Princess Juliana Airport on the Dutch side. Many people arrive on St. Martin by boat, as many cruise ships stop here. These visitors invariably arrive on the Dutch side of the island, as the port of Philipsburg is the only one large enough to receive cruise ships.

By Plane

Princess Juliana Airport

Most visitors arriving by plane land at the Princess Juliana Airport (Dutch side), which has all the necessary facilities to welcome them: a long runway located at the end of the beach of Maho Bay, duty-free shops, restaurants and car-rental companies. This place is always busy.

General Information:
☎*(599-5) 54.211*

Flight information:
☎*(599-5) 52.161*

Several airlines have offices here:

Air Canada: ☎*542-3316*
Air France: ☎*545-4212*
American Airlines: ☎*545-2040*
Continental: ☎*545-3444*
KLM: ☎*545-2120*
Winnair: ☎*545-4237*
AOM: ☎*545-4344*

If you want to rent a car, several companies have counters at the airport. All are located at the airport's exit (see p 120), and they all want to rent you a car, so you can try to negotiate, although it is hard to get any deals during the high season, when things are at their busiest. It is a good idea to reserve in advance.

The airport is located 10km from Philipsburg and 8km from Marigot. One road leads to both these cities. To reach Philipsburg by car, turn right when leaving the airport. There are two possible routes for Marigot. You can take the road toward Philipsburg, where after a few kilometres you'll come to another road that cuts into the interior and leads right to Marigot. The other way is to turn left when exiting the airport towards Terres Basses; this road leads directly to Marigot. Few vehicles take the second route, which is actually very easy.

You can also take a taxi to Marigot. Remember that taxis do not have meters, and that there are fixed rates to get around the island. For example to get from the airport to Marigot or Philipsburg costs US$8.

Finally, small buses run everywhere on the island, and will get you from the airport to Philipsburg for US$1.50. Once in Philipsburg, you'll have to take another bus to Marigot (another US$1.50). Departures are about every 10min.

L'Espérance Airport

L'Espérance Airport (French side) can only accommodate small planes (those serving other Caribbean islands) and is not nearly as busy as Princess Juliana. In fact, everything here closes at certain times. You can get flight information by calling ☎05.90.87.53.03.

If you are heading to St. Barts, it may be preferable to fly from this airport, which is less busy than the Juliana Airport on the Dutch side. The wait at the check-in desk is shorter, and the place is much calmer overall. Furthermore, air fare is much cheaper. However, this airport offers fewer services.

Several airline companies have counters here:

Air Caraïbes
700 F return (to St. Barts)
☎05.90.87.70.40

St. Barth Commuter
500 F return (to St. Barts)
☎05.90.27.54.54

You can also rent a car (see p 74) at the airport. Chances are you will leave the island of St. Martin from Princess Juliana Airport. Thus, it is wise to check if you can leave your car there, even if you rented it at L'Esperance Airport.

The airport is about 1km from Grand Case and 5km from Marigot. To get to either town, take the main road heading west.

By Boat

Several cruise lines criss-cross the Caribbean, making stopovers in Sint Maarten. Ships dock at the port of Philipsburg where you can shop on bustling Front Street or enjoy one of the beautiful beaches of the area.

Getting to St. Barts

The island of St. Barts only has one airport and can only handle small planes. Thus, travellers from North

America or Europe will usually arrive at Sint Maarten or Guadeloupe and then change to a smaller plane. Boaters can use the port of Gustavia on St. Barts, which is equipped to receive cruise ships despite its small size.

By Plane

Even though it is tiny, the **St. Barts Airport** offers all the services of an international airport, including customs, car rental agencies and a small restaurant. Travellers can get flight information by calling ☎05.90.27.65.41, or by calling the airlines directly.

The following airline companies have offices at the airport:

Air Caraïbes
☎05.90.82.47.00

St. Barth Commuter
☎05.90.27.54.54

Winnair
☎05.90.27.61.01

Visitors who want to rent a car won't have any problem because many car rental companies have counters at the airport (See p 142 in the St. Barts chapter).

There are no shops in the airport. There is, however, a shopping centre in front of the airport with a bank and some shops (perfume, alcohol, etc.)

The airport is about 2km from Saint-Jean and Gustavia. If you have rented a car or scooter, turn left as you exit the parking lot to reach Saint-Jean, and right to reach Gustavia.

You can also take a taxi, since there is a depot at the airport. Call ☎05.90.27.75.81 to reserve one.

Finally, there is no public transportation on the island. Besides taxis or a rental cars, the only options are walking and hitchhiking.

By Boat

Several Caribbean cruise lines stop in St. Barts. Cruise ships dock at the port of Gustavia. From there you can shop or enjoy one of the beautiful beaches of the area.

Between St. Martin and St. Barts

If you have a free day, you might consider an excursion to St. Barts (or St. Martin). Since the islands are only about 30km apart, many companies offer such trips. By plane or by boat, this is a great way to spend the day (especially heading

Table of distances (km)

Via the shortest route

©ULYSSES

Example: The distance between Colombier and Gustavia is 4 km.

St. Barts

	Colombier	Grand Cul-de-Sac	Gustavia
Grand Cul-de-Sac	9		
Gustavia	4	8	
Saint-Jean	4	5	3

St. Martin

	Baie Orientale	Grand Case	Marigot
Grand Case	5		
Marigot	10	5	
Philipsburg	8	13	8

from St. Martin to St. Barts by boat), what with the beautiful scenery and the exciting crossing.

Boats leave daily from Philipsburg (Bobby's Marina) in Sint Maarten or from the the port of Gustavia, in St. Barts, and take about 90min to make the crossing. The seas are often quite high (especially in the summer), and the trip can be rough for those with queazy stomachs (bring along some motion sickness pills). Seafaring types will find the crossing spectacular and enjoy every minute. **Gustavia Express** *(departures from l'Anse Marcel, ☎05.90.27.54.65)*, **Voyageur I** and **II** *(departures from Marigot and Philipsburg; Marigot ☎05.90.87.10.68, St. Barts ☎05.90.27.54.10)* and **The Edge** *(departures from Philipsburg, ☎544-2640)* are among the companies offering this trip out of St. Martin for US$50 or US$80 with lunch and a tour of St. Barts. Tickets are available at a stand at the entrance to Bobby's Marina (Philipsburg). Out of St. Barts, similar trips cost - 270 F and are offered by **Gustavia Express** *(☎05.90.27.19.83)*.

By plane, the trip takes 10min, during which time a small twin-engine plane takes you for a stable ride (relatively speaking) across the ocean. Departures are from the Princess Juliana and L'Espérance airports. There are several daily flights between the two islands, but it is nonetheless advisable to reserve in advance, particularly if you wish to leave on a particular day and time. The return trip costs approximately US$150 from Princess Juliana Airport; from Grand Case, the return trip costs 500 to 700 F, depending on the airline. Air Guadeloupe, Air Caraïbes, St. Barth Commuter and Winnair offer this service.

Schedules vary from one airline to another. Be aware, however, that the first flight departs around 7am and the last one around 5:15pm. It is always wise to reserve in advance.

Saint-Martin

Air Caraïbes
☎***05.90.82.47.00***

St. Barth Commuter
☎***05.90.27.54.54***

Winair
☎***05.90.29.19.11***

Sint Maarten

Air Caraïbes
☎***545-4212***

Winair
☎***545-4237***

St. Barts

Air Caraïbes
☎***05.90.27.61.90***

St. Barth Commuter
☎***05.90.27.54.54***

Winnair
☎***05.90.27.61.01***

Insurance

Before your departure, it is a good idea to inform yourself about the various types of insurance you may need. Take the time to compare prices and conditions from the various companies offering such insurance.

Cancellation

Cancellation insurance is usually suggested by the travel agent when you buy your airline ticket or tour package. It allows you to be reimbursed for the ticket or trip if your vacation must be cancelled due to serious illness or death.

Theft

Most house insurance policies in North America protect some of your goods from theft, even if the theft occurs outside the country. To make a claim, you must fill out a police report. In general, the amount of coverage provided for theft while travelling is about 10% of your total coverage. It may not be necessary to take out further insurance, depending on the amount covered by your current house insurance policy. Luggage insurance is recommended for European travellers.

Health

Before leaving, it is strongly recommended that you verify that you are adequately insured in case you should become ill. It is easy to purchase health insurance before leaving. Your insurance plan should be as complete as possible because health care costs can increase rapidly in St. Martin and St. Barts. These islands only have small clinics, and serious injuries or illnesses are generally treated in Guadeloupe, which often results in high transportation costs. Thus, it is important to make sure your policy includes such extra costs.

When buying insurance, make sure it covers all types of medical costs, such as hospitalization, nurse's services and doctor's fees. Make sure your limit is high enough, as these fees are expensive. A repatriation clause is also a good idea in case the required care is not available on site. Furthermore, you may have to pay these costs before leaving the clinic; verify what your policy provides for in this case. During your vacation, keep proof of your insurance policy on you, so that you can avoid any problems if you need it.

Health

You can rest easy in the knowledge that, no matter what happens, you will be given quality medical care when visiting St. Martin and St. Barts, and that the pharmacies are numerous and sell the latest medications. It is not necessary to protect yourself against any infectious diseases before travelling to St. Martin or St. Barts. Only those arriving from areas infected with yellow fever must be vaccinated against it.

A small first-aid kit can help you avoid many difficulties; prepare it carefully before leaving on your trip. Ensure that you have enough of all your regular medications, as well as a valid prescription in case you lose this supply. Other medication, such as Imodium or an equivalent, should also be bought before leaving. In addition, bring adhesive bandages, disinfectants, analgesics, antihistamines, an extra pair of glasses and pills for upset stomach.

Of course these islands are not worry-free when it comes to your health. Their two greatest attributes, the sun and the food, can also cause problems for tourists. Digestive problems, involving diarrhea and fever, do occur. If you get diarrhea, soothe your stomach by avoiding solids; instead, drink carbonated beverages, bottled water, or weak tea (avoid milk) until you recover. If the symptoms persist, see a doctor.

The sun's benefits are many, but so are its dangers. Always wear sunscreen (SPF 15 for adults and 25 for children) and apply it 20 to 30 minutes before exposure. Many creams on the market do not offer adequate protection; ask a pharmacist. Too much sun can cause sunstroke (dizziness, vomiting, fever, etc.). Be careful, especially the first few days, as it takes time to get used to the sun. A parasol, a hat and a pair of sunglasses are useful accessories for any day at the beach.

Insects are abundant everywhere on the islands and can be quite unpleasant. They are particularly numerous during the rainy season. To minimize the chances of being bitten, cover yourself well, avoid brightly coloured clothing, do not wear perfume, and use a good insect repellent. Remember, insects are more active at sundown. When walking in the mountains and forest areas, wear shoes and socks that protect your feet and legs. It is also advisable to carry ointments that will soothe the irritation caused by bites. Coil repellents will allow you to enjoy evenings on a terrace and in your room with the windows open.

You must also be careful to avoid coming into contact with the **manchineel tree**. This tree of the genus Euphorbia produces a poisonous sap that causes serious burns. It has been systematically removed from the beach areas but a few remain in certain places. Most of these have been marked by a red stripe of paint or a sign. The trees are recognizable by their small round leaves with a yellow central vein. Both the tree trunk and the leaves are dangerous, so do not touch them. Avoid using them for shelter during rain showers because the drops of rainwater carry the poisonous sap and can burn you. Furthermore, eating the fruit of this tree is also dangerous. If you do sustain a burn from this tree, or eat the fruit, consult a doctor immediately.

The water is potable throughout St. Martin and St. Barts.

Climate

The average temperature in St. Barts and St. Martin is 26°C. The heat is never stifling as regular breezes and trade winds come from the east and northeast. There are, however, still two seasons; the dry season, from November to April, and the rainy season, from May to October. The dry season is the more pleasant of the two because the heat is less intense, there is less rain, and the humidity is lower. The average temperature during this season is 24°C during the day, and 19°C at night. Travelling during the rainy season is also possible because even though rain showers are heavy, they do not last long. There is more rain from August to October. This is also hurricane season. During the rainy season, expect the temperature to hover around 27°C during the day and 22°C at night. The average hours of sunshine remain constant throughout the year.

Weather forecasts are available by calling:

in Saint-Martin
☎08.36.68.97.10

in Sint Maarten
☎545-4228

in St. Barts
☎05.90.27.60.17

Packing

The type of clothing required does not vary much from season to season. In general, loose-fitting, comfortable cotton clothes are the most useful. Closed shoes that cover the entire foot are preferred for walking in the city because they protect against cuts that might become infected. Bring a sweater or long-sleeved shirt for cool evenings, and rubber sandals to wear at the beach and in the shower. An umbrella is useful during the rainy season. Bring more dressy clothes if you anticipate evenings out. Finally, if you plan on doing some hiking, bring along appropriate footwear.

Safety

Like everywhere, there is a risk of theft in St. Martin (less so in St. Barts). A certain amount of caution can help pre-empt any potential problems. It is in your best interest to avoid taking out all your money when buying something and to leave nothing of value visible in your car.

A money belt can be used to conceal cash, traveller's cheques and your passport. That way, if your bags should happen to be stolen, you will at least have money and the necessary documents to help you out. Remember that the less attention you draw to yourself, the less chance you have of being robbed.

If you bring valuables to the beach, be sure to keep a constant eye on them. It is safer to keep your valuables in the small safes available at most hotels.

Transportation

St. Martin's road network is easy to sum up: basically one road skirts the island, and another one links Marigot and Philipsburg. There are also a few smaller roads, sometimes unpaved, that lead to some of the beaches. Relatively few cars travel these thruways, but traffic is nevertheless often heavy at the entrance to Philipsburg. The speed limit is usually 90 km/h on these roads (110 km/h in certain places).

St. Barts, with its 25km^2 of terrain, has a limited road network that is nonetheless quite sufficient for its inhabitants. There is little traffic on the roads, most of which are paved (except a few roads leading to quieter beaches), and often narrow and bumpy. Getting around by car is very easy.

Driving Tips for St. Martin and St. Barts

It is easy to find your way around the islands. Signs are generally clear and reliable, so reaching the centre of all the towns and villages is not a problem, although some areas in the Dutch half of St. Martin are not as well indicated.

Most roads are not well lit and often wind their way through hills, so be careful when driving at night.
Do not forget that you must give right of way to traffic coming from the right. This means that at intersections, you must yield to the car on the right no matter who got there first.

Be careful when approaching speed bumps, especially on St. Martin, where they have been placed on the outskirts of towns and near resort areas. They are usually well marked, and most are painted yellow. Some, however, are poorly marked. To avoid any unpleasant surprises, slow down when travelling through towns especially near the touristy areas like Baie Nettlé and Mullet Bay. To make travelling throughout the islands easier, buy the IGN (Institut Géographique National) map of Guadeloupe, with a 1:100,000 scale. There is also a more precise map of St. Martin and St. Barts with a 1:25,000 scale.

There are gas stations throughout St. Martin. The price of gas is about on par with average North American prices, a little less expensive on St. Barts. Most stations accept credit cards.

Renting a Car

There are car-rental agencies in the Princess Juliana, L'Espérance and St. Barts airports, as well as in most resort areas. Wherever you go, you can expect to pay about US$60 for an economy car and US$80 or more for an all-terrain vehicle (unlimited mileage) per day, not counting insurance and taxes.

In St. Barts, most agencies rent the same two types of vehicles: all-terrain types (Suzukis) or MOKEs, cute little topless cars that are perfect for drives along the coast. Expect to pay at least 300 F per day during the high season.

When renting a car, it is recommended that you take out automobile insurance to cover all costs in case of an accident. If you are paying by credit card, don't forget that certain gold cards offer automatic accident insurance if you use them to pay for your rental car. Before signing the contract, make sure that payment details are clearly defined. Your credit card must be able to cover the rental costs as well as the insurance deductible when you sign the contract.

A valid drivers' license from your home country is acceptable. You must be 21 years of age to rent a car. If you are travelling during the busy season, make sure to reserve your vehicle in advance.

Renting a Bicycle or a Scooter

If the open road beckons, it is easy to rent a motorcycle, a scooter or a bicycle. A scooter costs approximately 150 F per day and a bicycle 60 F per day. You will need to leave your drivers' license as a deposit, as well as 300 F when renting a scooter. Remember to drive carefully, and that wearing a helmet is obligatory. St. Martin's sunny roads and St. Barts's steep hills might discourage more casual cyclists.

St. Martin

Eugène Moto
Marigot
☎***05.90.87.13.97***

Rent a Scoot
Baie Nettlé
☎***05.90.87.20.59***

St. Barts

Barth'Loc
Gustavia
☎***05.90.27.52.81***

Chez Béranger
Gustavia
☎***05.90.27.89.00***

Fredo Moto
Rue Courbet, Gustavia
☎***05.90.27.67.89***

Taxis are one of the most efficient ways of getting around St. Martin. No meters are used, and all the rates are fixed (and non-negotiable, by the way). Here are a few sample rates:

Marigot - Baie Nettlé	US$10
Marigot - Grand Case	US$8
Marigot - L'Espérance airport	US$8
Marigot - Oyster Pond	US$20
Marigot - Philipsburg	US$8
Philipsburg - Orient Bay	US$15
Philipsburg - Mullet Bay	US$8
Princess Juliana Airport-Baie Nettlé	US$17
Princess Juliana Airport-Grand Case	20$US

On St. Barts, taxis can be found near the marina in Gustavia and next to the airport in Saint-Jean. You can also get one by calling:

Gustavia:
☎***05.90.27.66.31***

Airport:
☎***05.90.27.75.81***

Buses

There is no public transportation system on St. Martin. The buses that traverse the island are run by several private operations, and they do not serve the whole island. For example, there is no bus to Terres Basses. Essentially these buses are good to get from Mullet Bay to Philipsburg, from Philipsburg to Orient Bay, from Philipsburg to Marigot, and from Marigot to Grand Case. It is an efficient and inexpensive way to get around (as long as you want to get to one of these places). The buses are identified by small signs in their windshields that list the places they stop. There is no public transportation available on St. Barts.

Hitchhiking

For many locals, hitchhiking is the easiest way to get around (especially between cities not served by buses). When travelling short distances, people will often hitch a ride while waiting for a bus (just in case). This usually works well. However, a certain degree of caution is advised for women travelling alone. Hitchhiking is also an option on St. Barts. Remember, however, that in certain areas, cars pass very infrequently and 32 it can be faster to walk since distances are short.

Money and Banking

Currency

Three different currencies can be used on St. Martin: the U.S. dollar, the French franc, and the Dutch guilder. Francs are only accepted on the French side, and guilders only on the Dutch side (pretty strange on an island that for the most part does not have a border-crossing). So don't try to pay in francs in Philipsburg or in guilders at L'Espérance. If you are staying only in the Dutch zone, bring only U.S. dollars instead of worrying about two currencies. However, if you are staying in Saint-Martin, you have the choice between francs or U.S. dollars. Wherever you stay, bring some of both currencies in case you decide to visit the other side, and remember that the international airport is in Sint Maarten.

For certain foreign travellers, notably Canadians, it may be more profitable to pay in francs than in US dollars (depending on the exchange rate, of course). It is thus a good idea to check the exchange rates each time you change money. The French franc is the official currency on St. Barts, but several merchants also accept US dollars.

The prices given in this guide are in US dollars for Sint Maarten and in French francs for Saint-Martin and St. Barts.

Banks

In Saint-Martin, most banks can exchange foreign currencies into francs, guilders (rarely used) and US dollars. They usually offer good rates. In Sint Maarten banks are open for transactions Monday to Thursday from 8:30am to 3:30pm, and until 4:30pm Friday. The bank at Princess Juliana Airport is open every day from 8:30am to 5:30pm. In Saint-Martin, banks are open from 8am to noon and 2pm to 4pm. There are also automated teller machines (ATMs).

On St. Barts, there are banks near the airport and in Gustavia. All of them can change foreign currencies into francs or U.S. dollars. They are generally open from Monday to Friday, from 8am to noon and 1pm to 5pm.

Banks close at noon the day before legal holidays on both islands. Nevertheless, many of them have ATMs so it is always easy to make withdrawals.
Most bank machines accept Visa and MasterCard for cash advances; North Americans with bank cards that work with the Cirrus, Interac or PLUS systems can also withdraw money from instant tellers at any time. These machines can be found in a few cities, in particular Pointe-à-Pitre, Gosier and Saint-François. It is the fastest and easiest way to withdraw money, which is given to you in French francs. Service charges are usually withdrawn from your account for each transaction, but the exchange rates usually prove to be a little better.

Currency Exchange

You can also change your money at currency exchange offices. The rates are sometimes not as good, but there is no commission charged. Large hotels also change money. However, rates are worse than at banks or currency exchange offices.

Traveller's Cheques

It is always best to keep most of your money in traveller's cheques. Get your cheques in US dollars if you will be visiting Sint Maarten, and in French francs if you will be visiting Saint-Martin or St. Barts. Always keep a copy of the serial numbers of your cheques separate from the cheques, in case they are lost, so that the company can easily and quickly cancel the old cheques and replace them.

Credit Cards

Most credit cards, especially Visa, MasterCard, and American Express (in that order) are accepted in many businesses, including hotels and restaurants. While the main advantage of credit

Exchange Rates*

US$1	=	$1.57 CAN
US$1	=	1.10 EURO
US$1	=	£ 0.68
US$1	=	2.15 DM
US$1	=	10.55 Swedish Kronor
US$1	=	2.42 Guilder
US$1	=	8.18 Danish Kroner
1 FF	=	$0.23 CAN
1 FF	=	$0.16 US
1 FF	=	0.15 EURO
1 FF	=	£ 0.09
1 FF	=	0.30 DM
1 FF	=	0.34 guilder
1 FF	=	1.46 Swedish Kronor
1 FF	=	1.13 Danish Kroner
$1 CAN	=	US$0.64
1 EURO	=	US$0.91
£ 1	=	US$1.47
1 DM	=	US$0.46
1 Kronor	=	US$0.09
1 Guilder	=	US$0.41
1 Kroner	=	US$0.12
$1 CAN	=	4.32 FF
$1 US	=	6.34 FF
1 EURO	=	6.56 FF
£ 1	=	10.60 FF
1 DM	=	3.35 FF
1 guilder	=	2.98 FF
1 Kronor	=	0.68FF
1 Kroner	=	0.88 FF

* Samples only, rates fluctuate

cards is that they allow you to avoid carrying large sums of money, using a credit card also makes leaving a deposit for a rental car much easier. In addition, the exchange rate with a credit card is usually better. However, do not count on using them everywhere, and always make sure you have some cash with you. Credit cards also let you avoid service charges when exchanging money. By overpaying your credit card (to avoid interest charges), you can then withdraw against it. You can thus avoid carrying large sums of money or traveller's cheques. Withdrawals can be made directly from an automated teller if you have a personal identification number (PIN) for your card.

Cheques

Visitors, even those from France, should not count on paying with personal cheques, since many businesses do not accept them because of the risk of fraud.

Automated Teller Machines (ATMs)

Banks on St. Martin (Dutch and French sides) as well as St. Barts offer ATM service for cash withdrawals. Most are members of the Cirrus and PLUS networks, which allow visitors to make direct withdrawals from their personal accounts. You can use your card as you do normally—you'll be given U.S. dollars with a receipt, and the equivalent amount will be debited from your account. All this will take no more time that it would at your own bank! That said, the network can sometimes experience communications problems that will prevent you from obtaining money. If your transaction is refused by the ATM at one bank, try another bank where you might have better luck. In any case, be careful not to find yourself empty-handed. Note that in French territory (Saint-Martin, St. Barts), ATMs provide cash in Francs, while on the Dutch side, cash is provided in US dollars.

Mail and Telecommunications

Telecommunications offices from which you can make long-distance calls can be found in Marigot, Philipsburg and Gustavia. These offices also sell phone cards to be used in public telephone booths. These cards come in two denominations in Saint-Martin: 36 F and 87 F. In Sint Maarten there is only one, which costs US$9.95.

Emergency Telephone Numbers

Saint-Martin	Ambulance: ☎05.90.87.86.25 Hospital: ☎05.90.29.57.57 Police: ☎05.90.87.50.04
Sint Maarten	Ambulance: ☎130 Hospital: ☎111 Police: ☎543-1111
St. Barts	Hospital ☎05.90.27.60.35 Police: ☎05.90.27.66.66

The area code for Dutch Sint Maarten is now 599. Note that this area code was recently changed and that all numbers start with 54.

In France, changes in the telephone system oblige you to add 05.90 before every number in French Saint-Martin and St. Barts, whether you are calling from within this area or from another French territory. From anywhere else, dial 590.

To Call from Saint-Martin

To Sint Maarten
00 + 599 + 54 + the five-digit phone number

To St. Barts
Dial the 10-digit phone number

To Canada and the United States
001 + area code + the number you are calling

To Great Britain
00 + 44 + the number you are calling

To Call from Sint Maarten

To Saint-Martin or St. Barts
00 + 590 + the six-digit number you are calling.

To Canada and the United States
001 + area code + the number you are calling

To Great Britain
00 + 44 + the number you are calling

To Call from St. Barts

To Saint-Martin
Dial the 10-digit phone number

To Sint Maarten
00 + 590 + 54 the five-digit number you are calling

To Canada and the United States
001 + area code + number you are calling

To Great Britain
00 + 44 + the number you are calling

To Call from the United States and Canada

To Saint-Martin and St. Barts
011 + the 10-digit number of your correspondent, omitting the first 0

To Sint Maarten
011 + 5995 + the number you are calling

To Call from Great Britain

To Saint-Martin and St. Barts
00 + the 10-digit number you are calling, omitting the first 0

To Sint-Maarten
00 + 5995 + the five-digit number you are calling

Calling Home

There are two ways to call long distance from the islands. The first option is to place a direct-dial call, which is charged according to local telephone rates. To call North America, dial 00, then 1, then the area code and the phone number. To call overseas, dial 00, the country code (see below), then the telephone number.

Country Codes

Great Britain:	44
Netherlands:	31
Australia:	61
New Zealand:	64
Belgium:	32
Italy:	39
Switzerland:	41
Germany:	49
Canada:	01

The second option for calling long distance from the islands is to use the operator and pay the rates of the country which you are calling. The following access numbers will connect you with operators in your home country:

Canada Direct: 0-800-99-00-16

AT&T Direct: 0-800-99-00-11 (from French Saint-Martin and St. Barts); 001-800-872-2881 (from Dutch Sint Maarten)

MCI Direct: 0-800-99-00-19 (from French Saint-Martin and St. Barts); 001-800-888-8000 (from Dutch Sint Maarten)

Post offices have fax and telex machines.

Travelling with Children

Travelling with children, however young they may be, can be a pleasant experience. A few precautions and ample preparations are the keys to a fun trip.

Aboard the Airplane

A good folding stroller will allow you to bring an infant or small child everywhere you go and will also be great for naps, if needed. In the airport, it will be easy to carry with you, especially since you are allowed to bring the stroller up to the plane's entrance.

Travellers with children can board the plane first, avoiding long line-ups. If your child is under the age of two, remember to ask for seats at the front of the plane when reserving your tickets since they offer more room and are more comfortable for long flights, especially if you've got a toddler on your lap. Some airlines even offer baby cribs.

If you are travelling with an infant, be sure to prepare the necessary food for the flight, as well as an extra meal in case of a delay. Remember to bring enough diapers and moist towels, and a few toys might not be a bad idea!

For older kids who might get bored once the thrill of taking off has faded, books and activities such as drawing material and games will probably do the trick.

When taking off and landing, changes in air pressure may cause some discomfort. In this case, some say that the nipple of a bottle can soothe infants, while a piece of chewing gum will have the same effect on older children.

In Hotels

Many hotels are well equipped for children, and

there is usually no extra fee for travelling with an infant. Many hotels have cribs; ask for one when reserving your room. You may have to pay extra for children, however, but the supplement is generally low.

Car Rentals

Most car rental agencies rent car seats for children. They are usually not very expensive. Ask for one when making your reservation.

The Sun

Needless to say, a child's skin requires strong protection against the sun; in fact, it is actually preferable not to expose toddlers to its harsh rays. Before going to the beach, remember to apply sunscreen (SPF 25 for children, 35 for infants). If you think your child will spend a long time under the sun, you should consider purchasing a sunscreen with SPF 60.

Children of all ages should wear a hat that provides good coverage for the head throughout the day.

Swimming

Children usually get quite excited about playing in the waves and can do so for hours on end. However, parents must be very careful and watch them constantly; accidents can happen in a matter of seconds. Ideally, an adult should accompany children into the water, especially the younger ones, and stand farther out in the water so that the kids can play between the beach and the supervising adult. This way, he or she can quickly intervene in case of an emergency.

For infants and toddlers, some diapers are especially designed for swimming, such as "Little Swimmers" by Huggies. These are quite useful when having fun in the water!

Accommodations

Luxurious and comfortable hotels abound on St. Martin and St. Barts. Staying on the cheap, however, can be quite a challenge. The Association des Gîtes de France, a French bed and breakfast association, does not have any members on the island, and there are very few "budget hotels."

We have listed what we believe to be the best accommodations, keeping in mind the price category, location and particular advantages of each one.

Time Sharing

While strolling on the island of St. Martin, particularly the Dutch side, you will undoubtedly notice a few places that resemble resorts but have a sign that says "private club." Though they are indeed private, you will be invited to visit one of these places on more than one occasion during a simple jaunt to Marigot or Philipsburg. These clubs, in fact, offer an innovative accommodation formula: the time-share option. If you agree to visit them you will be "treated" to — or sometimes actually pressured into attending — a sales-pitch session during which you will be offered, not the outright purchase of a flat, but simply the opportunity to "own" it for one week per year. Love it or hate it, the fact remains that there are dozens of these complexes on the island. If you are not interested, refuse any invitation and abstain from participating in any contest entitling you to attend. Note, however, that you can sometimes lease one of these apartments without being a member; simply inquire within.

All the prices mentioned in this guide apply to a standard room for two people in the high season. The various services offered by each establishment are indicated with a small symbol. In no case is this an exhaustive list of what the establishment offers, but rather the services we consider to be the most important. Please note that the presence of a symbol does not mean that all the rooms have this service; you sometimes have to pay extra to get, for example, a fireplace or a whirlpool tub. And likewise, if the symbol is not attached to an establishment, it is probably because the establishment cannot offer you this service. However, please note that unless otherwise indicated, all hotelsin this guide offer private bathrooms. For a guide to the symbols used, please see the key in the first few pages of the guide. Prices indicated were valid at press time, and apply to a standard room for two people during the high season (January to April). They are of course subject to change at any time. For Saint-Martin and Sint Maarten, a **5% tax** is added to the rates cited in this guide. St. Barts, of course, is tax-free.

Restaurants

Excellent restaurants of all kinds are plentiful on the island of St. Martin, especially on the French side. From small French bistros to restaurants serving refined French cuisine or exotic specialties, not to mention the little food stands along the beach specializing in seafood and grilled fish, there is a spot to suit everyone's taste.

Meanwhile, St. Barts has several fine dining establishments, pleasant bistros that serve French and Creole dishes, and cafés where you can stop in for a sandwich or some ice cream. Whatever your tastes, you will eat well on either island!

In an effort to satisfy the needs of all our readers, we have sampled and tasted throughout the island in order to offer a selection of restaurants for all budgets. A phone number and address is included for each establishment, where possible.

The price indicated is the price of a meal for one person, excluding drinks and tip.

$	less than 60 F
$$	60 F to 125 F
$$$	125 F to 200 F
$$$$	more than 200 F

$	less than $US 10
$$	$US 10 to $US 20
$$$	$US 20 to $US 30
$$$$	more than $US 30

Calendar of Events

Various festivals are celebrated throughout the year, with parades, dancing, music and games of all sorts. Below is a list of some of the more noteworthy events.

• St. Barts's international music festival has been held every January for more than 10 years.

• Carnival is celebrated on both islands but at different times, leading to double the fun. In Saint-Martin and St. Barts, it starts a few day before Shrove Tuesday (*Mardi Gras*) and ends on Ash Wednesday (*Mercredi*

Holidays

All banks and businesses are closed on public holidays. Be sure to change money and do your shopping the day before. In the following list (F) indicates a holiday on the French side, and (D) a holiday on the Dutch side.

January 1 (F/D)	New Year's Day
Variable (F)	Shrove Tuesday (*Mardi Gras*)
Variable (F/D)	Ash Wednesday
Variable (F/D)	Easter Sunday and Monday
April 30 (D)	Queen's birthday
May 1 (F/D)	Labour Day
May 8 (F)	Remembrance Day Armistice 1945
Variable (F/D)	Ascension Day
May 27 (F)	Abolition of Slavery
Variable (F)	Whitsun
July 14 (F)	National Holiday
July 21 (F)	Victor Schœchler Day
August 15 (F)	Assumption
August 24 (F)	Fête de Saint-Barthélemy (St. Barts)
November 1 (F)	All Saints' Day
November 11 (F)	Remembrance Day Armistice 1918
November 11 (D/F)	St. Martin Day
December 25 (F/D)	Christmas

des Cendres) when the carnival effigy is burned. In Sint Maarten, the carnival takes place during the last two weeks of April. Among the activities are the elections of a Carnival queen and a Calypso king.

• The waters off Sint Maarten fill with colourful yachts for the Heineken regattas in March.

• July 14 is the French national holiday and a time for parades, sports competitions and fireworks, both in Saint-Martin and St. Barts.

• Schœlcher day, which commemorates the emancipation of the slaves, is celebrated on July 21 in Grand Case.

• The Fête de Saint-Barthélemy takes place on August 24 and is a perfect opportunity to celebrate and organise regattas, games and races. The next day, August 25, Saint Louis is celebrated in Corossol.

• November 11 sees parties throughout the island of St. Martin to mark St. Martin Day.

Miscellaneous

Electricity

As in continental Europe, appliances work on 220 Volts (50 cycles). Even though there are a few 110-Volt plugs, North Americans should bring along a converter and an adapter.

Women Travellers

Women travelling to these islands don't need to worry: life is peaceful and violence is infrequent. Of course, the usual amount of caution should be exercised.

Time Difference

St. Barts and St. Martin are on Eastern Standard Time. However, there is no daylight savings time, so in winter the islands are one hour ahead of New York and Montréal. There are five hours of difference between the islands and Greenwich Mean Time during the summer and four hours in the winter.

Accommodations on Saint Martin, such as this one, are each more lavish than the last. - *L.P.*

Some pristine white sand beaches with turquoise water remain on Saint Martin.
- L.P.

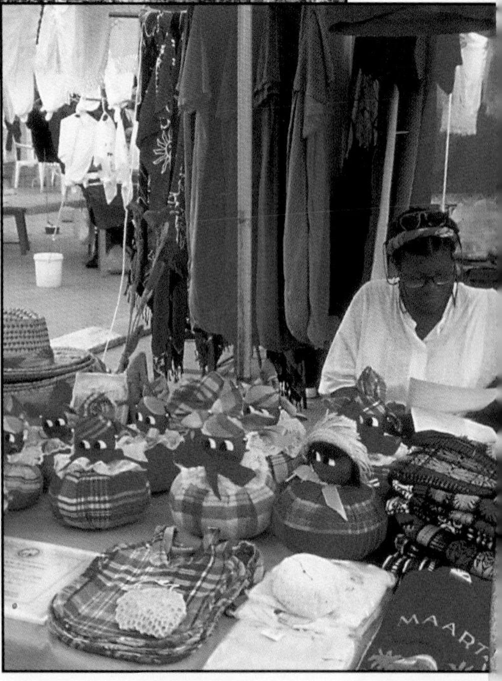

Dolls clothed in madras, a traditional Antillean fabric, are sold at the market in Marigot.
- L.P.

Outdoors

Whether you want to ride the waves, discover underwater treasures or relish the beach from beneath the shade of a beach parasol, the islands of St.Martin and St. Barts are sure to please.

And while the beaches of the former are among the prettiest in the Lesser Antilles, the latter will charm you with its lovely and quiet coves. Whatever your sport or activity, a little preparation will go a long way toward helping you make the most of your excursions.

Swimming

Ahhh, the sea... crystal-clear, refreshing waters and waves perfect for all types of activities—an integral part of any vacation. Remember, though, that the better one understands the sea, the better one is able to enjoy it. More specifically, beaches on the islands' leeward side (Caribbean Sea) are less exposed to the wind, so the waters are much calmer; these are perfect spots for family swimming. Beaches on the windward side (Atlantic Ocean) are rougher and will please visitors in search of big waves.

There are no private beaches on either St. Martin or St. Barts, so you can swim anywhere you like. However, certain beaches are difficult to access because they lie behind the property of huge resorts that do not allow the public onto their grounds. Nothing stops you from frequenting these beaches; just remember that most of the hotel facilities adjoining them are reserved for hotel guests, so try to stick to the beach.

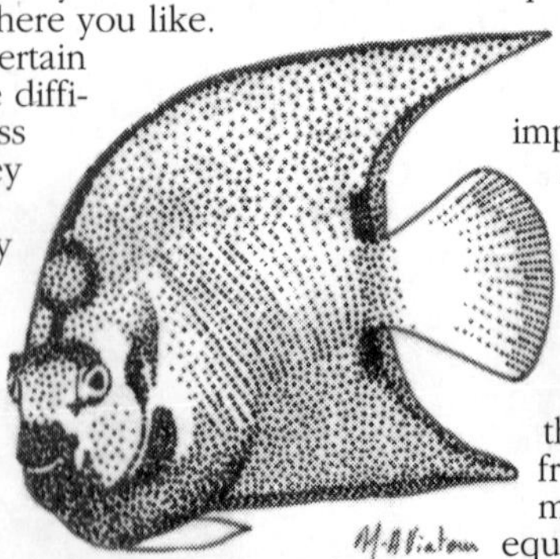

Angelfish

Scuba Diving

There are many diving centres throughout the islands that offer divers the chance to explore the ocean floor surrounding St. Martin and St. Barts. Certified divers can explore the secrets of these coastlines to their heart's content. Novices can also embark on underwater explorations, but must be accompanied by a qualified guide who will supervise their descent (to a maximum depth of 10 to 15 m). The sport is not dangerous; just be sure that the supervision is adequate. Before taking your first plunge, it is very important to at least take an introductory course in order to learn basic safety skills: how to clear the water from your mask, how to equalize the pressure in your ears and sinuses, how to breathe underwater (don't hold your breath) and become comfortable with the change in pressure underwater, and to familiarize yourself with the equipment. Many hotels offer a resort course of about 1hr for first-timers. Equipment can easily be rented from the different centres along the coasts.

Scuba diving lets you discover fascinating sights like coral reefs, schools of multicoloured fish and amazing underwater plants. Don't forget that this ecosystem is fragile and deserves special attention. All divers must respect a few basic **guidelines** in order to protect these natural sites: do not touch anything (especially not urchins, as their long spikes can cause injury); do not break off pieces of coral (it is much prettier in the water than on land, where it becomes discoloured); do not disturb any living creatures; do not hunt; do not feed the fish; be careful not to disturb anything with your fins and, of course, do not litter. If you want a souvenir of your underwater experience, disposable underwater cameras are available.

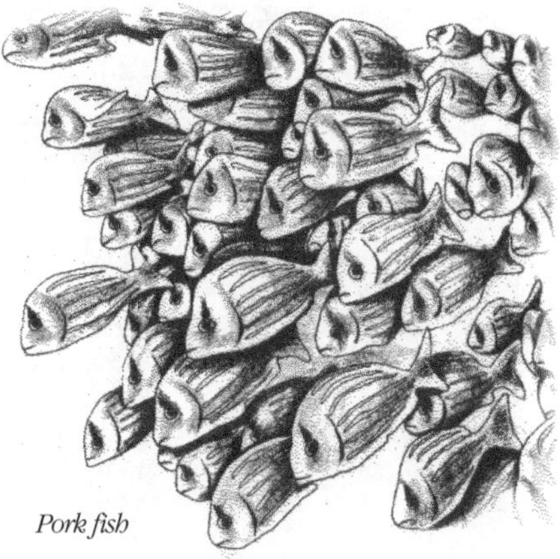
Pork fish

Snorkelling

If you are drawn to the sea, but not interested in diving, snorkelling is the perfect alternative. It doesn't take much to snorkel: a mask, a snorkel and some fins. Anyone can enjoy this activity, which is a great way to appreciate the richness of the underwater world. Not far from several beaches, you can go snorkelling around coral reefs inhabited by various underwater species. Some companies organize snorkelling trips. Remember that the basic rules for protecting the underwater environment (see scuba diving section) must also be respected when snorkelling.

Parasailing

Another unusual way to enjoy the vast expanse of the ocean is to view it from above, by parasailing! Securely attached to your parachute and tied to a powerful motorboat, you are hoisted up into the air in seconds. Once airborne, you have 10min or so to enjoy the spectacular bird's-eye view of your surroundings. Not for the faint of heart.

A Fragile Ecosystem

Coral reefs are formed by minuscule organisms called "coelenterate polyps," which are very sensitive to water pollution. The high level of nitrates in polluted water accelerates the growth of seaweed, which in turn takes over the coral, stops it from growing and literally smothers it. Sea urchins (whose long spikes can cause severe injuries) live on the coral and play a major role in controlling the amount of seaweed that grows on the coral by eating what the fish cannot. An epidemic threatened the survival of many reefs in 1983, when the waters became so polluted that sea urchins were affected and seaweed flourished in the Caribbean Sea. Scientific studies have since proved the importance of urchins to the ecological balance, and the species has thus been restored on certain reefs. However, these little urchins cannot solve the problem on their own. Pollution control is essential if the coral reefs, upon which 400,000 organisms depend, are to survive.

Windsurfing

Several of the islands' beaches are washed by calm waves, which might not suit seasoned sailboarders, but are ideal for the less experienced.

The only beach on the islands that has some serious wind and waves for windsurfing is the one at the **Baie de l'Embouchure**. Less experienced boarders can enjoy practising in more controlled conditions at other locations.

Deep-Sea Fishing

Deep-sea fishing excursions offer the excitement of a big catch on the high seas and make for a fun outing besides. These trips usually last half a day. Equipment and fishing tips are provided by the organizers.

Personal Watercraft

These high-speed contraptions that fly across the water provide thrills and hours of entertainment for many travellers. Learning to manoeuver them takes little time, and reasonable caution should be exercised at all times to avoid an accident. If you are careening about, always yield the right of way to slower and less easily manoeuvrable boats (sailboats, pedal-boats, etc.), and watch out for swimmers and divers. The latter are often hard to spot, but the boat accompanying them always flies a red flag with a white line through it when the divers are down. Never approach these boats when this flag is flying.

Hiking

Though the islands are tiny and do not have any national parks, you can still head off on foot along the hills of St. Barts (there is only one trail, in the **Colombier** region) or up to the top of **Pic Paradis** (400m) on St. Martin. These hiking trips hold many surprises, but require some preparation in order to avoid problems associated with the hot tropical sun (see below). And though the distances are short, it is a good idea to know the level of difficulty and change of altitude of the trail you plan on hiking and to stick to the trail.

Sunstroke

Long sections of exposed trail mean that all hikers run the risk of sunstroke. Dizziness, nausea, cramps and goose bumps are the first symptoms. Anyone experiencing these symptoms needs immediate shade, water and ventilation. To avoid the problem, always wear a hat and a good sunscreen. By getting an early start, you'll have time for a day hike in cooler temperatures.

Clothing

The general rule is to wear lightweight and light-coloured clothing. Thick-soled shoes that are lightweight and solid with good traction are the best. Also, bring a raincoat to keep you dry in case of rain and a hat to protect you from the sun.

What to Bring?

A daypack with a pocket knife, antiseptic, bandages, adhesive bandages, scissors, Aspirin, sunscreen, insecticide, food and above all enough water for the trip should be brought on every hike, regardless of the duration.

Bicycling

The steep, hilly and sunny roads of St. Martin and St. Barts are not ideal for leisurely bike rides. There are, however, several smaller roads that lead to the islands' beaches, so short rides are possible. Bikes can be rented at different points around the island. Expect to pay about 60 F per day (see p 54).

Horseback Riding

St. Martin and St. Barts have a few riding stables that organize excursions for enthusiasts of this sport, offering a pleasant way to discover the island.

Golf

There is only one golf course on the island of St. Martin, at **Mullet Bay**. Unfortunately, most of its facilities, including the buildings of the Mullet Bay Casino and Resort, were severely damaged by Hurricane Luis in 1995. Though repairs have been made and it has reopened to golfers, the terrain remains in a sad state. The buildings are supposed to be redone, but no date has been mentioned. There are no golf courses on St. Barts.

Saint-Martin

The French part of the island of St. Martin measures just 55km², in which are located the elegant city of Marigot and some charming villages.

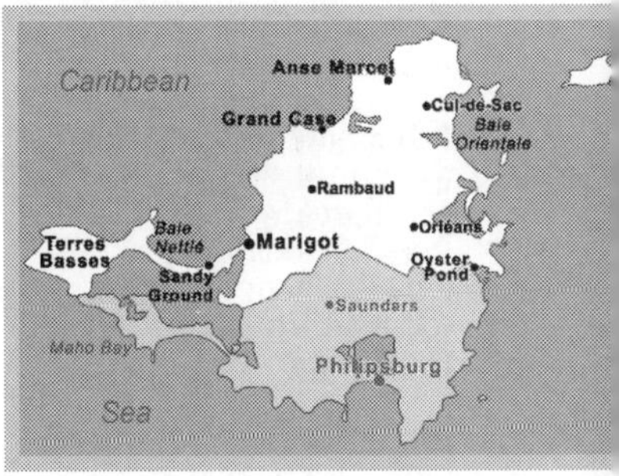

The territory is, in fact, a microcosm of France in the middle of the Caribbean; there are a number of good restaurants, shady terraces which make wonderful places to watch the world go by, and some Parisian-style boutiques. At the same time, this land is very Caribbean, with coasts punctuated by long crescents of fine sand, swept by the trade winds and lush, verdant gardens where a multitude of flowering plants grow.

Whether you amble through one of the island's charming and authentic villages, such as Grand Case, which have managed to combine Creole life with a holiday ambiance, or whether you prefer entertainment, seaside terraces or the upscale boutiques of Marigot, Saint-Martin truly has something to please everyone.

Finding Your Way Around

By Car

A single main road, in very good condition, runs through the whole French part of the island. From **Marigot**, this road travels east to **Orient Bay**, passing through **Grand Case** on the way. Heading west, the same road goes through **Terres Basses**, making its way to Sint Maarten, the Dutch part of St. Martin. By taking this road, travellers will easily reach the **L'Esperance airport in Grand Case** to the east, or the **Princess Juliana airport** to the west.

A section of road running inland also links **Marigot** to **Philipsburg**. To take this road from **Marigot**'s downtown area, you must follow Rue de Hollande to the junction with the main road, which leads toward **Philipsburg**.

A few secondary roads, most of which are well paved, go to villages and isolated beaches such as Anse Marcel and Friar's Bay.

Road signs are clear and reliable.

Renting a Car

L'Espérance Airport

Avis
☎*05.90.87.50.60*

Hertz
☎*05.90.87.73.01*

Sanaco Car Rental
☎*05.90.87.14.93*

Thrifty
☎*05.90.87.26.50*

Marigot

Avis
☎*05.90.87.50.60*
⇄*05.90.87.97.66*
www.avis.com

Budget
⇄*05.90.87.38.22*

Europcar
☎*05.90.27.32.80*
⇄*05.90.87.55.23*

Hertz
☎*05.90.87.40.68*
⇄*05.90.87.75.47*

Island Trans Rent a Car
☎*05.90.87.91.32*
⇄*05.90.87.70.87*

Thrifty
☎*05.90.29.24.24*
⇄*05.90.29.24.79*

Baie Nettlé

Budget
☎*05.90.87.21.91*

Hertz
☎*05.90.87.33.71*

By Bus

Marigot Bus Station

Corner of Rue Président Kennedy and Rue de Hollande.

Grand Case

You can catch a bus to Marigot on the main road downtown, or right on the

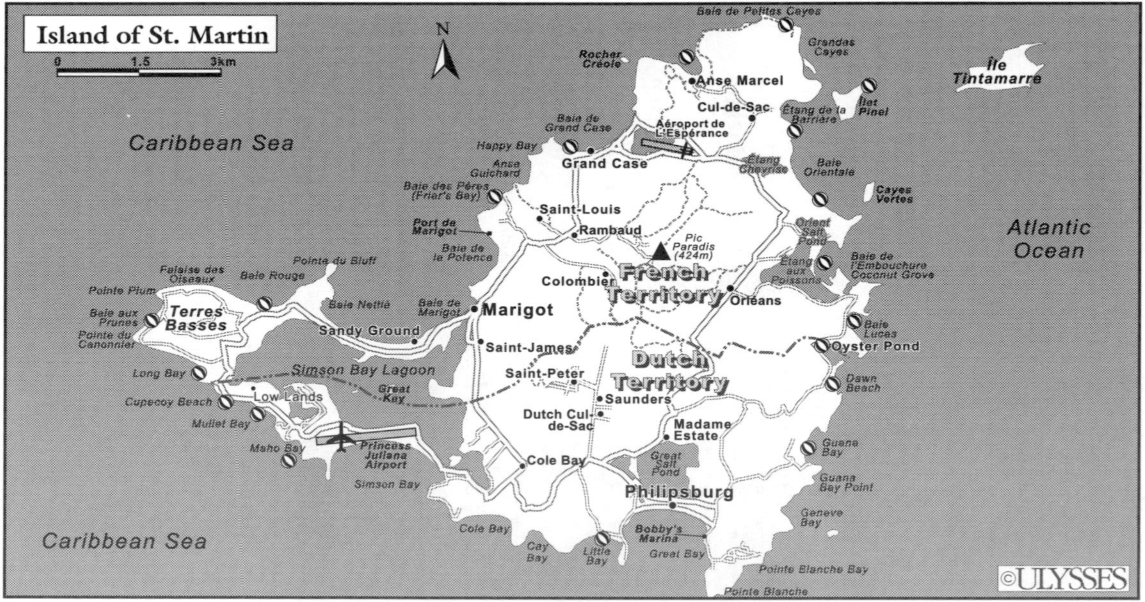
Island of St. Martin
0
1.5
3km
N
Caribbean Sea
Caribbean Sea
Atlantic Ocean
Île Tintamarre
Baie de Petites Cayes
Grandes Cayes
Rocher Créole
Anse Marcel
Cul-de-Sac
Étang de la Barrière
Îlet Pinel
Baie de Grand Case
Aéroport de L'Espérance
Happy Bay
Grand Case
Étang Chevrise
Baie Orientale
Anse Guichard
Baie des Pères (Friar's Bay)
Cayes Vertes
Saint-Louis
Port de Marigot
Rambaud
Orient Salt Pond
Pic Paradis (424m)
Baie de la Potence
Étang aux Poissons
Baie de l'Embouchure
Coconut Grove
Pointe du Bluff
Falaise des Oiseaux
Baie Rouge
Colombier
French Territory
Pointe Plum
Orléans
Baie Nettlé
Baie de Marigot
Marigot
Baie aux Prunes
Terres Basses
Pointe du Canonnier
Sandy Ground
Saint-James
Baie Lucas
Oyster Pond
Dutch Territory
Long Bay
Simson Bay Lagoon
Saint-Peter
Dawn Beach
Great Key
Low Lands
Cupecoy Beach
Saunders
Dutch Cul-de-Sac
Mullet Bay
Madame Estate
Princess Juliana Airport
Maho Bay
Guana Bay
Great Salt Pond
Cole Bay
Simson Bay
Guana Bay Point
Philipsburg
Geneve Bay
Cole Bay
Bobby's Marina
Cay Bay
Little Bay
Great Bay
Pointe Blanche Bay
Pointe Blanche
©ULYSSES

main road at the city's entrance.

By Taxi

☎*05.90.87.56.54*

Practical Information

Tourist Information

Route de Sandy Ground
97150 Marigot
☎*05.90.87.57.23*
⇄*05.90.87.56.43*
www.st-martin.org

Banks

Banque des Antilles Françaises
Rue de la République, Marigot
☎*05.90.29.13.30*

Banque Commerciale Française
☎*05.90.87.53.80*

Currency Exchange Bureaus

Change Point
Rue du Président Kennedy, Marigot
☎*05.90.87.24.85*

Inter Change
Rue du Général de Gaulle, Marigot
☎*05.90.87.73.41*

Change Plus
15 Rue de la Mairie
☎*05.90.87.30*

Post Offices

Saint-Martin has post offices in Marigot, Grand Case and Baie Nettlé. If you do not wish to go all the way there, note that certain hotels also offer mail service.

Marigot

Mon-Fri 7:30am to 4pm, Sat 7:30am to 11:30am
Rue de la Liberté
☎*05.90.87.53.17*

Grand Case

Mon-Fri 7:30am to 4pm, Sat 7:30am to 11:30am
Boulevard Laurence
☎*05.90.87.05.96*

Medical Care

Hospital

Marigot Hospital
☎*05.90.29.57.57*

Ambulance

Day: ☎*05.90.87.86.25*
Night: ☎*05.90.87.72.00*

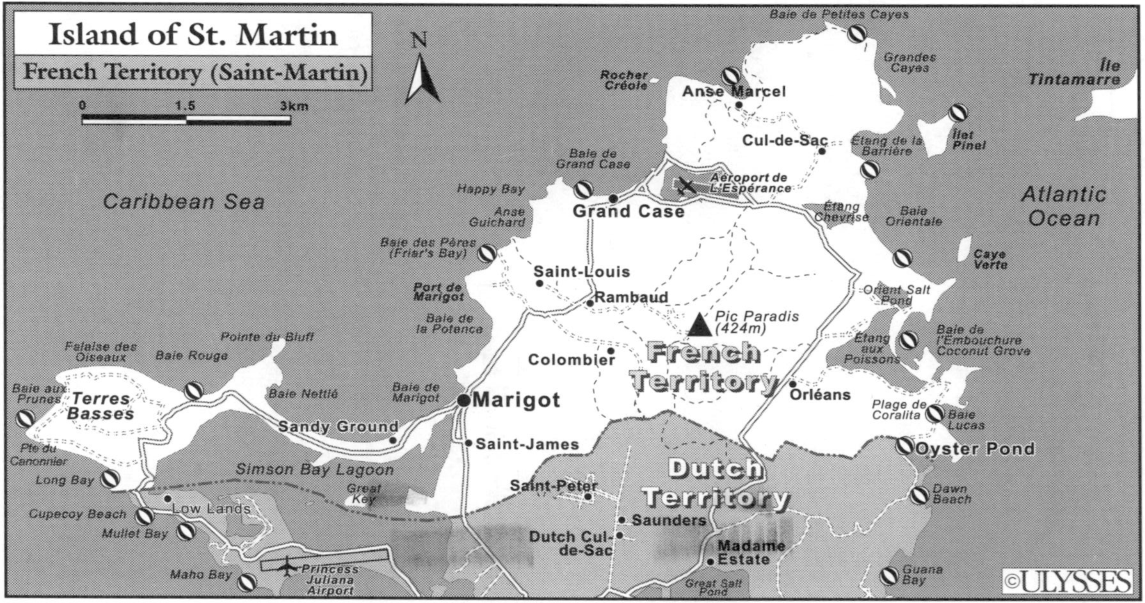

Island of St. Martin
French Territory (Saint-Martin)
N
0
1.5
3km
Caribbean Sea
Atlantic Ocean
Baie de Petites Cayes
Grandes Cayes
Île Tintamarre
Rocher Créole
Anse Marcel
Îlet Pinel
Cul-de-Sac
Étang de la Barrière
Baie de Grand Case
Aéroport de L'Espérance
Happy Bay
Grand Case
Étang Chevrise
Baie Orientale
Anse Guichard
Baie des Pères (Friar's Bay)
Caye Verte
Saint-Louis
Port de Marigot
Rambaud
Orient Salt Pond
Pic Paradis (424m)
Baie de la Potence
Baie de l'Embouchure Coconut Grove
Étang aux Poissons
Falaise des Oiseaux
Pointe du Bluff
Baie Rouge
Colombier
French Territory
Baie aux Prunes
Terres Basses
Baie Nettlé
Baie de Marigot
Marigot
Orléans
Plage de Coralita
Baie Lucas
Sandy Ground
Saint-James
Oyster Pond
Pte du Canonnier
Simson Bay Lagoon
Dutch Territory
Long Bay
Great Key
Saint-Peter
Dawn Beach
Low Lands
Cupecoy Beach
Saunders
Mullet Bay
Dutch Cul-de-Sac
Madame Estate
Maho Bay
Princess Juliana Airport
Guana Bay
Great Salt Pond
©ULYSSES

Pharmacies

Pharmacie du Port
Rue de la Liberté, Marigot
☎05.90.87.50.79

Pharmacie La Lagune
Résidence La Lagune, Baie Nettlé
☎05.90.87.20.00

Pharmacie de Grand Case
Route de la Déviation, Grand Case
☎05.90.87.77.46

Attractions and Beaches

The towns and villages of Saint-Martin are certainly charming enough to hold anyone's attention, and a visit to the most beautiful among them is highly recommended. This Caribbean island's main attraction, however, is its beaches; long golden crescents of sand, bordered by azure waters, are strewn all along the coast. From Marigot, a tour through this French land, its villages and natural treasures will offer visitors an incomparable experience.

Marigot

Marigot ★★, the main town in Saint-Martin, is located on the north shore of the island, on a point of land that was one of the first areas to be colonized, thanks to its proximity to a large bay. Baie de Marigot is protected from strong winds, making it perfect for mooring boats. Though the site was advantageous for sailors, it did pose a few problems for colonists, since the Baie de Marigot was not always rimmed with sand as it is today. Originally, it was surrounded by mangroves and swampland, hence its name, which means "backwater" in French. This vegetation proved a real nuisance for colonists, who could neither cultivate nor pass through this area. They were forced to eliminate it in order to access the waters of the bay more easily.

Nature was not the only concern of the colonists of Marigot; right from the beginning, the village had to contend with attacks by the English. Starting in 1666, French authorities contemplated building a fort in order to protect the colony. It was not until 1767, however, that construction of **Fort Saint-Louis ★★** *(free admission; reached by following Rue de l'Église)* began.

Marigot
ACCOMMODATIONS
1. Hôtel Beach Plaza
2. Le Patio
3. Marina Royale
4. Royal Louisiana
RESTAURANTS
1. Bar de la Mer
2. Belle Époque
3. Boulangerie-Charcuterie
4. Brasserie de la Gare
5. Chanteclair
6. Charolais
7. Délices de France
8. La Vie en Rose
9. Le Saint-Germain
10. Mini-Club
N
Fort Saint-Louis
Baie de Marigot
Sandy Ground, Baie Nettlé
Boul. de France
parking lot
public market
Rue de l'Église
H
Rue de la Liberté
Rue de la République
Rue Fichaut
Rue Félix Éboué
Rue du Palais de Justice
Rue de l'Anguille
courthouse
Rue Maurasse
city hall
Rue de l'Hôtel de Ville
Rue du Général de Gaulle
Rue Président Kennedy
Rue St-James
Rue de Hollande
Simson Bay Lagoon
Marina Port La Royale
Philipsburg
Grand Case
0
60
120m
©ULYSSES

The project was conceived by the Chevalier Descoudrelles, a knight who sought to take advantage of the hills surrounding the bay. The fort was built on the summit of these hills and commands a full view of the bay. Construction was completed in 1789 under Descoudrelles's successor, Durat. A few years later, in 1794, the English troops conquered the magnificent, strategically placed stone structure. The fort remained in their possession until the island was liberated a few years later by Victor Hugues (see p 26). After the Treaty of Vienna (1815), English attacks ceased and the fort was gradually abandoned. Today, its ruins still dominate the city. Visitors can tour the site and enjoy the superb **view** ★ from on high.

The city of Marigot consists of a lower and an upper part. Visitors touring the lower part of the city can explore the developed area around the fort or take a leisurely tour of the hillside, with its lovely Creole cottages and beautiful colonial homes with elaborate balconies. The town has experienced gradual expansion and new districts have developed, first to the east of the fort (where a high school was built), then around the ocean, in an area once covered by an insalubrious swamp that was filled around 1965. Today, visitors will see the beautiful Port la Royale marina here, as well as modern buildings housing boutiques and restaurants. All this makes the place ideal for enjoying a bite to eat while observing the comings and goings of boats, whose lovely colours brighten the horizon.

Between the fort and the Port la Royale marina is

Marigot's downtown area, which occupies the area between Rue du Général de Gaulle and the outskirts of Baie de Marigot. This is where the majority of boutiques and restaurants are located, and visitors are sure to be charmed by the peaceful activity reigning throughout. A stroll through the streets of downtown should lead you to the edge of the bay, where you can spend hours contemplating the beautiful spectacle of the shimmering waves while sitting on a park bench or at a table on one of the inviting terraces, judiciously set up here.

There is a large square facing this seafront where a **public market ★** is held every Wednesday and Saturday morning. Stalls move in and take over the area, proffering all sorts of goods, from spices to fragrant exotic fruits to cotton clothing and, of course, Creole crafts. Take the time to rummage and poke about for there are sure to be a few items to please you among this jumbled pile of merchandise. A feast for the eyes, this market will delight even those who do not wish to purchase anything.

The upper part of the city extends over the west side of Marigot's hill, where the residential district of Saint-James stands, set back from the town and isolated due to its dense vegetation.

To leave Marigot, take Rue de la Liberté, which becomes the island's main road.

A museum has opened its doors next to Marigot: **Sur les Traces des Arawaks ★★** *(US$5; 9am to 1pm and 3pm to 7pm, closed Sun; ☎05.90.29.22.84)*. This museum recounts the history of the island's very first inhabitants, the indigenous Arawak-speaking peoples who arrived here over 3,500 years ago. Several pieces, notably seashell tools, pottery shards and mother-of-pearl jewellery, discovered during archaeological digs executed on the island, are exhibited. Each object is accompanied by a host of information about these people, allowing visitors to better understand their way of life and their beliefs. Museums dedicated to the Arawaks are rare, so this is a good opportunity to learn more about these people who were destroyed following the arrival of the first European colonists. A second room presents the life of the inhabitants of Saint-Martin at the turn of the 20th century. This fascinating trip through time is illustrated with black-and-white images depicting everyday scenes from that era and these photographs are all the more interesting as they are often paired with others portraying the same scene today.

Those who would like to find out more about the archaeological excavations being conducted in Saint-Martin can go to the **Parc Archéologique de Hope Estate** *(by guided tour only, ☎05.90.29.22.84)*. Many of the Arawak artifacts displayed at the museum were found on this very site.

Terres Basses

On the way out of Marigot, heading west, you'll arrive at **Sandy Ground**, which is actually an extension of the city. A few restaurants and beaches make up the bulk of this hamlet, which is the gateway to the **Terres Basses**, or lowlands, a narrow strip of land in the shape of a loop leading to the Dutch side of the island. Several tourist villages have been constructed on these lowlands, where one shore gives onto the Caribbean Sea and the other onto the Simson Bay Lagoon. One of these is located at **Baie Nettlé**, alongside some stunning **beaches** ★. Some of the most beautiful resorts on the French side of the island are found here (see p 19). Each comprises comfortable buildings, housing both rooms and restaurants. Things are much quieter in these isolated establishments than in the village of Mullet Bay.

This part of the island is sparsely inhabited, save for these tourist areas and a scattering of opulent residences that stand high in the hills, enabling their residents to enjoy superb views of the crystalline waters of the sea. These houses can only be admired from afar, but no matter: the big attraction here is the beautiful beaches, which are among the best on the island.

The first beach you'll encounter coming from Marigot is the one at **Baie Rouge** ★★. It is accessible via a short dirt road that opens up onto a parking lot for cars, motorbikes and hotel tour buses (this spot is very popular). At this point, a trail a few metres long is all that separates you from the beach. Follow it and you'll find yourself at the edge of the sea on a beautiful fine-sand beach bounded by steep cliffs atop which stand some of Saint-Martin's luxurious residences. This is a wonderful place to soak up some rays. Unfortunately, slippery rocks lie along parts of the shore and swimmers must use caution to get beyond them. Also, the waves are often strong. A small drink stand and picnic tables have been set up for the public.

The beach at **Baie des Prunes** ★ is another 2km farther along. Pay close attention, because a small sign indicating *"baignade non-surveillée"* (unsupervised swimming) is all that marks the trail leading to the beach. Bound by sea-grape trees growing haphazardly here and there, the beach seems deserted, lending it a certain charm. However, a short stroll along this long ribbon of soft, fine sand reveals beautiful residences hidden behind luxuriant vegetation. Slippery rocks are a nuisance here as well.

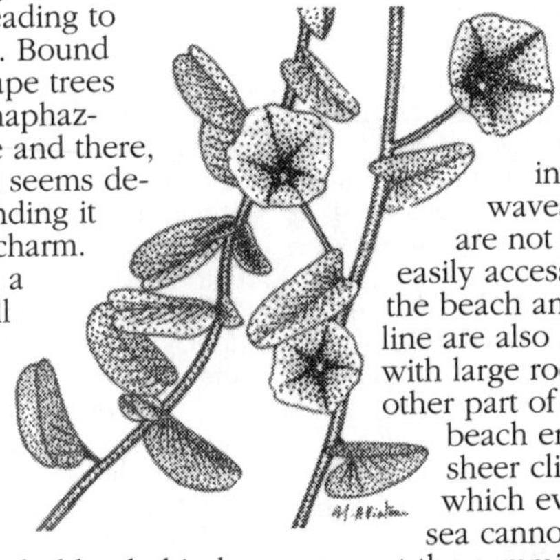

The sheer cliff known as **Falaise aux Oiseaux** marks the northern extremity of the beach. Lovely homes perched atop its summit overlook the azure waters. At the southern extremity of the beach is a path leading to Long Bay and passing through **Pointe du Canonnier**.

A third beach extends along the lowlands. As its name suggests, the beach at **Long Bay** ★★ is the longest, but it is also the prettiest of the three. This beach could be divided into two distinct parts. The first, which lies farther west, has a wild appearance, much like the beach at Baie aux Prunes. Not very developed and bordered by rather wild vegetation, this beach is caressed by the ocean's inviting waves, which are not always easily accessible, as the beach and shoreline are also strewn with large rocks. The other part of the beach ends in sheer cliffs, which even the sea cannot conquer, at the summit of which stand the magnificent buildings of the La Samanna hotel (see p 95). The beach at the foot of these cliffs is more inviting to swimmers.

Around Pic Paradis

To reach the eastern part of the island from Marigot, follow Rue de Hollande, which leads to the main road.

The road heads east and follows the coast for a while before leading inland. About 2km out of Marigot, you'll cross a dirt road weaving its way between Creole cottages to the seaside at **Friar's Bay** ★ (Baie des Pères). This isolated beach, bordered by palm trees, is washed by perpetually calm waters, making it a favourite with swimmers who prefer to avoid big waves. The beach also scores points with snorkellers, who come to explore the beautiful coral reefs offshore. Lined with a few beach restaurants, it attracts a young vacationing clientele with its beautiful beach and "cool" ambiance.

On the way back to the main road, you'll pass another road on your right barely 100m after Friar's Bay. It is very narrow and climbs up a hill to Colombier.

Colombier

The tiny hamlet of **Colombier**, with its mere handful of humble abodes scattered here and there, remains unadulterated and far from the tourist villages. A stroll down its only street is like stepping into another world. Besides its Caribbean cachet, though, the village has little to offer.

It is, however, of undeniable interest to travellers heading off on the **Sentier des Crêtes**. To reach this trail, take the road at the entrance to the village all the way to the end. You'll find a small pink house; the trail runs behind it, then continues on to St. Peters (Sint Maarten) and up Pic Paradis. If you hike the trail, make sure to bring enough water, as there is none available along the way or at the summit of Pic Paradis.

Many people choose to scale **Pic Paradis** (424m), but if this hike seems too arduous, you can always ascend by car. To do so, retrace your steps and follow the main road to Rambaud (1km). From there, follow the town road as it meanders up to the summit. The road is steep and uneven, and seems almost impassable at times, but the **view ★★** is stunning and well worth the effort. To get to the lookout, take the trail (which is in fact part of the "Route des Crêtes," see p 92) to the left of the France Télécom gates and follow it for some 10min. You will then reach a plateau where there are lookout points affording magnificent panoramas. Weather-permitting, you can even see some of the islets of the Caribbean chain in the distance.

By continuing on the main road towards Grand Case, you'll end up in Saint-Louis.

Saint-Louis

Stop in **Saint-Louis**, a small cliff-top village with just a

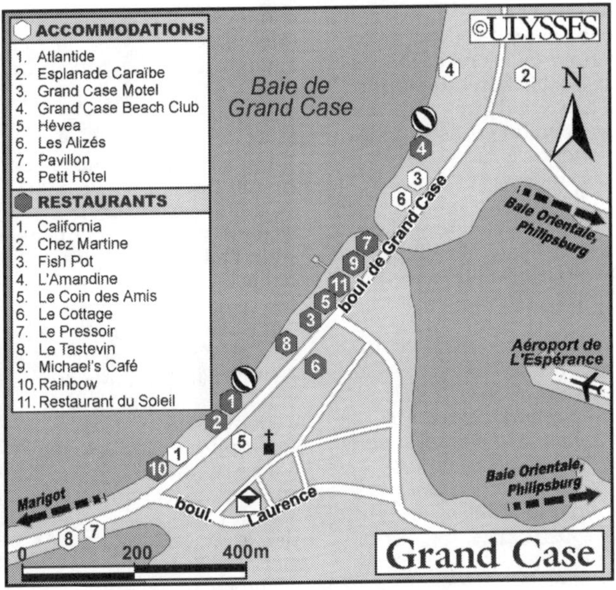

few houses, to take advantage of the spectacular **view** ★ of the coast. There is no real lookout point, so you'll have to stop by the side of the road to take it all in.

Grand Case

Grand Case ★★ is without a doubt the most picturesque village on the island. There are no luxurious mansions, just a charming, typically Caribbean village whose beauty lies in its simplicity and its pretty colours. Extending along the shore, Grand Case consists of a series of small, lovely Creole houses and emanates a wonderful holiday atmosphere. Residents live in harmony with the vast glittering expanse of sea, while visitors come to relax on the beautiful crescent of fine sand and contemplate the moored boats bobbing ever so gently in the calm waters. Don't forget the other reason people come to Grand Case: the excellent restaurants (see p 108)! All of these features make this a popular spot with vacationers.

Grand Case's charms are not all apparent to the naked eye, as some of them are more understated. Magical scenery lies concealed on the outskirts of the village. Offshore, the Caribbean Sea thrives with coral, multicoloured fish and a variety of plants—a veritable underwater paradise that visitors will have a chance to admire while diving. Several enterprises organize such excursions (see p 89).

If the depths beckon but the thought of scuba gear doesn't, reserve a spot on the **Seaworld Explorer ★** *(adults US$40/320 F, children US$20/160 F; departure from the pier at 11am, subject to change; 05.90.59.95.24. 078)*, a semi-submersible boat with passenger seats in the hold; you are thus sitting more or less under the boat, and explore the sea-floor 15m below the surface. There are large portholes so that you can view the natural wonders. It's quite a trip!

From Grand Case, follow the main road east. First you will come to L'Espérance airport, then a few hundred metres farther you will cross a secondary road cutting off to the left. Follow it to the fork and get into the left land, which goes to Anse Marcel.

Anse Marcel

The road cuts through steep hills and reveals several beautiful **panoramas ★**. Then around a corner magnificent **Anse Marcel ★** (*anse* means cove) appears. The town, nestled in verdant hills, extends along the sea and consists mainly of superb gardens and exquisite hotels (see p 100). A veritable haven of tranquility, far from all traffic and noise, the setting is truly exceptional.

This spot is not easy to reach, however, since Anse Marcel is not served by public buses; visitors will therefore have to get there on their own. Furthermore, no doubt to discourage trespassers, guards are posted at the entrance, monitoring the comings and goings of visitors.

There is a pleasant **beach ★** at Anse Marcel, but if isolated beaches are what you are looking for, follow the walking trail that starts at Anse Marcel and weaves its way through the foothills. It leads to the beautiful beach at **Baie des Petites Cayes**. This is the only way to reach this beach, except by boat.

The path continues, making its way to **Grandes Cayes ★**. Concealed behind the grass and shrub-covered hills, this beach, consisting of a few coves, is wild and not very busy; only sea-grape trees clutter its blond sand. The turquoise ocean stretches out as far as the eye can see. Travellers can also get there by taking the dirt road that leaves from French Cul-de-Sac and runs alongside the hills to Grandes Cayes. If you decide to visit this beach, bring your beach umbrella, as there is no shade.

French Cul-de-Sac

If you want to go to French de Cul-de-Sac, coming from Grand Case by the main road, take the secondary road to your left (the one that also leads to Anse Marcel) all the way to the fork. This time take the fork to the right.

A small road leads to the northernmost tip of the island, a virtually uninhabited region that receives little rainfall. It does, however, boast a few lovely, quiet coves. Moreover, this, or more precisely the Étang de la Barrière, is the point from which the boats leave for Pinel Island.

The **Étang de la Barrière** is unique because of the stunning green tint of its waters. Unfortunately, there is a lot of seaweed and rocks, which may be unappealing to some visitors. There is a parking lot and a few stands on its banks selling various souvenirs such as T-shirts, sarongs and sculptures. Most people stop here on the way to Îlet Pinel.

The outline of **Îlet Pinel ★** *(40 F return; 9:30am to 5pm)* is discernable off the shores of Baie de Cul-de-Sac. This tiny island is a great place to escape to, and enjoy the sandy beach and the sensation of being on a desert island far from the crowds. Chairs and beach umbrellas are available for rent. Water taxis shuttle passengers to the islet, leaving when full (generally every 20min) from the Étang de la Barrière quay. You can also get there directly from Orient Bay, though this costs a little more.

The beach at Baie Orientale is also the place from which water-taxis take visitors to **Île Tintamarre** *(US$10; every day, 7am to 5pm)*, located 2km off the coast. This island reserves some stunning underwater scenery for divers (see p 90).

Atlantic Coast

You can easily reach Orient Bay from the main road. Precise road signs show the way.

★★★ Orient Bay

If there's an image you'll cherish, it's bound to be of Orient Bay: a long ribbon of fine sand stretching out as far as the eye can see, bordered by the shimmering waves of the Atlantic Ocean. This beach, unquestionably the loveliest on the island, is perpetually crowded with visitors who come here to enjoy water sports or the pleasures of a delightfully refreshing swim, or simply to have their skin caressed by the hot rays of the sun (prudent sun bathers will have brought their own parasol). Merchants have set up shop, offering all kinds of merchandise, from souvenirs to sports equipment, beverages and food. Many will undoubtedly deplore this succession of unsightly stalls, which sticks out like a sore thumb in this otherwise magnificent tableau. Visitors will find consolation, however, in that this does little to mar the beach's unparalleled beauty.

The beach welcomes nudists. The approaches to the bay have been protected by a new park; this entire area, where several hotels have been erected, is now a protected zone.

By following the road toward Orient Bay, you will cross the town of Orléans, site of the home of Roland Richardson, a local painter.

On the outskirts of the same village, near the road, at the top of the cliffs that tower above the waves, is the **Old House Museum** *(every day 9am to 4pm, ☎05.90.87.32.67)*. This is the well-preserved great house of the sugar plantation Spring, the interior of which is now a rhum museum. The museum explains how rhum is produced from sugar cane juice, as well as a collection of rhums, instruments required for its production, and labels. It also presents the opportunity to discover a lovely period house and to get an idea of the way of life in the past.

Baie de l'Embouchure

Travellers continuing along the road will reach the Baie de l'Embouchure and the Étang aux Poissons. You will notice the mangrove

The St. Martin Nature Reserve

During the 1990s, the inhabitants' desire to create a nature reserve that would protect the fragile ecosystem along the coasts of St. Martin prompted the authorities to create the Réserve Naturelle de Saint-Martin. This reserve covers the coasts of the islets of Pinel, Tintamarre and Green Key (Caye Verte), the reefs of Creole Rock (Rocher Créole), located off the bay of Grand Case, as well as the coast of the Baie de l'Embouchure.

This reserve was created in order to protect the extremely high biodiversity of these areas. This includes, the coral reefs of the "côte-au-vent," which act like ramparts, protecting a rich aquatic life composed most notably of fish, spiny lobsters, crabs and shellfish. Between the coral reef and the coast, an underwater herbarium has developed, where algae shelters a variety of marine animals. The mangrove, another ecosystem necessary to the survival of a great many animal species, also benefits from this special protection. This damp, marshy area surrounds the Étang aux Poissons and is home to birds such as cattle and snowy egrets. It is also a favoured reproduction area for a number of fish. Finally, the reserve protects a large part of the shores and cliffs.

A marine park has also been created along the shores of the Dutch part of the island. Its purpose is to protect marine life and the fragile ecosystems of the zone located off the island, while at the same time regulating the diverse marine activities practiced by island residents.

swamp that has developed along the shores of the latter. This strange forest, looking much like an impenetrable tangle, is composed of mangroves, trees whose long aerated roots enable them to grow in mud and water. All of this rich ecosystem is now part of the Réserve Naturelle de Saint-Martin, which was created in 1998.

The beach on the Baie de l'Embouchure is hardly among the most beautiful on the island, but it is a favourable spot for windsurfers of all levels, as beginners will find its banks well-sheltered from the winds, and more seasoned enthusiasts can take advantage of the strong winds blowing across the open sea.

Not far from the Baie de l'Embouchure you will notice a long structure that houses an unusual and captivating attraction: the **Butterfly Farm** ★ *(US$10; every day 9am to 4pm; Le Galion Beach, ☎05.90.87.31.21).* Here you can discover the wondrous world of lepidopterans as you walk, accompanied by a guide, amongst an abundance of plants and several hundred freely fluttering butterflies representing some 20 species. Visitors will also be able to witness these insects' complete metamorphosis: caterpillars turning into cocoons, the development of pupae and the birth of multi-coloured butterflies. The tour lasts 20 to 25min.

Keep following the road until you arrive at Baie Lucas.

Baie Lucas

Baie Lucas (Coralita Beach) is situated north of Oyster Pond. This bay is not as busy as the other two, no doubt because its banks are covered in seaweed. It remains, nonetheless, a pleasant beach of white sand.

Travellers continuing south will end up in Sint Maarten, the Dutch part of the island (see p 119).

Outdoor Activities

Ribbons of fine white sand extend between land and sea at various points along the island's periphery. These beaches are a veritable paradise for water sports enthusiasts. Hikers will find their own small paradise along the trails that criss-cross the hills in the centre of the island. In fact, the island offers nature lovers a wide range of activities from which to choose.

This section provides information on how to go about practising those activities, as well as addresses of places that rent out sports equipment.

Swimming

The island's beaches, each one lovelier than the last, have something to offer every kind of swimmer. There is only one nudist beach among them; it lies at the southern extremity of Orient Bay.

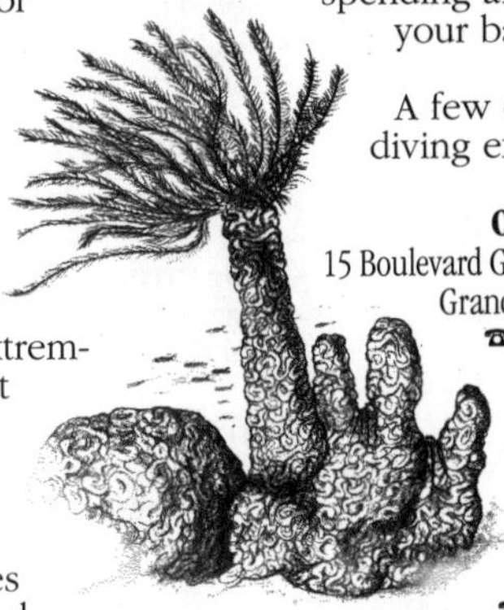

Descriptions of the best beaches can be found in the "Attractions and Beaches" section of this chapter.

Scuba Diving

Scuba-diving enthusiasts will not be disappointed, because the island boasts a number of interesting sites. Coral reefs have developed off the coasts of Baie de Marigot, Friar's Bay, Baie aux Prunes and Grand Case bay. In Saint-Martin, the **Creole Rock** is one of the favoured diving sites for beginners, since a multitude of fish as well as magnificent corals can be seen here in waters no more than 10m deep. Visitors can observe this wondrous world's fascinating underwater life by taking part in an excursion. Count on spending around 400 F for your baptism.

A few centres organize diving excursions:

Octopus
15 Boulevard Grand Case B.P. 072,
Grand Case 97070
☎***05.90.87.20.62***
⇄***05.90.87.20.63***

Blue Ocean
Centre Commercial
Baie Nettlé
Baie Nettlé 97060
☎***05.90.87.89.73***
⇄***05.90.87.26.36***

Sea Horse Diving
Coralia Mercure Simpson hotel beach
Baie Nettlé
☎***05.90.87.84.15***

Sea Dolphin
Flamboyant hotel beach, Baie Nettlé
☎***05.90.87.60.72***

Scuba Fun
Anse Marcel
☎***05.90.87.36.13***

The desert-like island of **Tintamarre** is especially renowned for its coral reefs; if this adventure sounds tempting, you can get there via several enterprises organizing excursions near this islet's coast, located 2km off the coast of St. Martin. The excursion includes the crossing by boat, a diving survey of the coral depths and a picnic on one of the island's beautiful beaches.

Seasoned thrill-seeking divers might prefer an excursion off the coast of **Saba** (Dutch Antilles), whose dive sites (for experienced divers) hold the enviable title of the most beautiful in the Caribbean.

Snorkelling

Most dive centres also organize snorkeling excursions. Count on spending about 50 F for equipment rental.

Blue Ocean
Centre commercial Baie Nettlé
☎***05.90.87.89.73***

At either end of **Orient Bay**, shopkeepers rent snorkeling equipment: 30 F per hour or 55 F per day.

Octopus
Grand Case
☎***05.90.87.20.62***

Parasailing

Off the beaches of Orient Bay and Baie Nettlé, visitors will soon catch sight of parasailing buffs executing dizzying flights while suspended between earth and sky. This experience is not restricted to the intrepid elite, and you too can take part (if you don't suffer from vertigo). A few centres organize such adventures:

Blue Ocean
Centre Commercial Baie Nettlé
280 F

Orient Bay
Stand at the edge of the beach
280 F (US$50)

Sailing

Sailing is another enchanting way to explore the sea's crystalline waves. Some centres organize excursions, while others rent out sailboats to experienced sailors.

Blue Ocean
Centre Commercial Baie Nettlé
sailboat rental (Sunfish): 550 F per half-day.

Club Nathalie Simon
Baie Orientale
☎*05.90.29.41.57*
(rental, instruction)

Windsurfing

Certain beaches on the island have won the favour of windsurfers, but only a few offer rollers and strong winds. In fact, the Baie de l'Embouchure beach may be the only one that is truly suited to this sport. Many, however, are ideal for beginners, and promise hours of fun. Baie de l'Embouchure, Friar's Bay, Orient Bay and Baie Nettlé are a few places where you can rent equipment and show off your skills.

Blue Ocean:
Centre commercial Baie Nettlé
rental: 140 F

Bikini Beach
Baie Orientale
rental: 100 F/hr

Windy Reef
Baie de l'Embouchure
☎*05.90.87.08.37*
rental 100 F/hr, 400 F /5hrs; courses also offered.

Kayaking

Some centres, particularly on the beach in **Orient Bay**, rent out kayaks that let you can skim over the waves. Count on spending 60F an hour.

Kontiki Watersport
Baie Orientale
☎*05.90.87.46.89*

Deep-Sea Fishing

Anglers interested in the deep-sea experience can check out the following establishments:

Blue Ocean
Centre Commercial Baie Nettlé
☎*05.90.87.89.73*

Hôtel Méridien
Anse Marcel
☎*05.90.87.67.00*

Personal Watercraft

Personal watercraft may be rented at:

Blue Ocean
Centre commercial Baie Nettlé

Sally's Jet Watersports
Orient Bay

Hiking

As is the case with a number of Caribbean islands, the towns and villages of St. Martin are scattered along its coasts, with very few hamlets in the heart of the island itself. This area, rather, consists of a small mountainous massif whose highest summit reaches 424m: **Pic Paradis**. Though very few roads lead to this peak, it is criss-crossed by many small paths, as the inhabitants prefer cutting through the island to get from one end to the other rather than going around. Many of these small paths, which actually only make up a single trail called **Route des Crêtes**, link St. Peters to Mont Vernon, passing Colombier and Pic Paradis.

Totalling no fewer than 40km, Route des Crêtes literally winds its way around the massif, revealing fabulous panoramas in various spots along the way. Open to all, this trail provides a good opportunity to discover St. Martin's back country. Hikers should come prepared, however, for the trail is long and offers very little shade (the island's vegetation is often limited and trees along the trail are few and far between), and neither water nor food are sold along most of the journey.

Although the trails are maintained, nature often gets the upper hand here, especially after rain showers, when it can become a little harder to find the trail. You should therefore stay alert and be careful to remain on the trail so as not lose your way. Some parts of the trail are marked with paint on tree trunks.

Other paths criss-cross the island, revealing fabulous views in places. One of them departs from Saint-Louis and reaches some lovely sea views in Friar's Bay. You can also take another one, which winds its way between hills along the coast from Grande Anse bay to the Baie de l'Embouchure, passing not far from Anse Marcel.

Bicycling

For all intents and purposes, the island has one road, which cars speed along. It winds through the hills, and uphill sections are often steep. Furthermore, it is generally unshaded.

There are also a few secondary roads, but you'll always have to take the main road to reach them. Bicycles are therefore not the ideal mode of transport on the island and few people use them. Bikes can nevertheless be rented at different places on the island. Expect to pay about 60 F per day.

Location 2 Roues
Baie Nettlé
☎05.90.87.25.59

Horseback Riding

A few riding stables organize tours, offering a pleasant way to discover the island.

OK-Corral
between the mouth of the Baie de l'Embouchure and Coralita Beach
☎05.90.87.40.72

Caïd et Isa
Anse Marcel
☎05.90.87.45.70

Bayside Riding Club
Baie de l'Embouchure
☎05.90.87.36.64

Accommodations

Marigot

Royal Louisiana
440 F, bkfst incl.
Général de Gaulle
☎/⇄05.90.87.86.51
There are a few hotels in Marigot, most of which offer an average level of comfort. Among them, the Royal Louisiana is worth mentioning. It is located right downtown and offers modest rooms.

Le Patio
520F
≡
corner of Rues Maurasse and de la République, 97150
☎05.90.29.12.32
⇄05.90.29.38.98
Also located in the city, Le Patio has tidy, comfortable enough rooms. Each of its 20 rooms is suitably furnished and has a private bath. Obviously, the tranquility of the beach is replaced with the liveliness of the city, but for those who prefer to stay in Marigot, this is a good choice.

Marina Royale
690 F
Rue St. James
☎05.90.87.52.46
If you want to stay in Marigot but also enjoy the

pleasures of being close to the sea, the Marina Royale hotel may be the perfect place. This tidy blue-and-white building has an enchanting site near the marina. Situated in the heart of the action, it offers decent rooms, some of which have a view of the marina.

Hotel Beach Plaza
1,600 F ocean view
≈, ≡, ℜ
Baie de Marigot, 97150
☎05.90.87.87.00
⇄05.90.87.18.87
www.hotelbeachplazasxm.com
A series of oceanfront buildings marks the entrance into Marigot. Among these is the blue-and-white Hotel Beach Plaza. Its delightful lobby, which pleasantly opens out onto the sea and boasts a magnificent view, leads to the rooms, some of which have a balcony overlooking the sea or the garden. These are, of course, the most prized, since the others have a less enviable view of the parking lot. However, all are comfortable.

Baie Nettlé

The western part of the island ends with a long, narrow strip of land that separates the Atlantic from the calm salty waters of Simson Bay Lagoon. This strip of land boasts several attractive beaches and offers views out over the very different stretches of water on either side. Luxurious hotels have been built on both the Dutch and the French side.

Long stretches of fine-sand beaches are found all over the western point, some washed by the bay, others by the Atlantic. Baie Nettlé is the first beach west of Marigot. Luxurious resorts have been built here and there.

Laguna Beach
550 F
≈, ≡, ℜ
97150
☎05.90.87.91.75
⇄05.90.87.81.65
The Laguna Beach faces the Royal Beach and offers similarly priced rooms of superior quality. The lobby is a large, somewhat inhospitable room. At one end is the restaurant, followed by the garden. The hotel boasts large, simply decorated rooms with pleasant balconies. It also comprises a lovely garden and a large swimming pool looking out on Simson Bay Lagoon.

Royal Beach
665 F, bkfst incl.
≈, ≡, ℝ
B.P. 571, 97056
☎05.90.29.12.12
Among the string of resorts, the Royal Beach, situated behind the Baie Nettlé shopping centre, stands out for its lower prices. Built by

the ocean, the hotel offers similar advantages to the other hotels in the area (a big pool, a beach, though it is a bit small, and a garden). Unfortunately, the building itself and the garden, which have both seen better days, are rather disappointing at first glance.

Nettlé Bay
940 F for a room in the gardens, bkfst incl.
≈, ℜ, ≡, *K*
B.P. 4081, 97064
☎05.90.87.68.68
The Nettlé Bay offers two types of accommodation: villas, which include one or two large rooms and a kitchenette, and the "gardens," which is a series of bungalows, each with 35 rooms. All of the buildings have been designed to afford a view of the bay and the pool from each room.

Mercure Simson
1,080 F bkfst incl.
≈, *K*, ≡, ℜ, ⊗
B.P. 172, 97150
☎05.90.87.54.54
⇄05.90.87.92.11
The Mercure Simson resort is made up of a number of buildings. The rooms each have a large balcony and a view of the bay. The balcony is almost like an extra room, since it is both useful (the kitchenette is there) and pleasant. Mornings and late afternoons spent here are particularly delightful. The complex also has a large garden planted with brilliantly flowering bushes and, of course, a pool around which most of the day's activities take place.

Flamboyant Resort
1,100 F +16%
≈, ⊛, ℜ, ≡, *K*
97150
☎05.90.87.60.00
Amongst the posh, comfortable hotels on the bay, the Flamboyant Resort, with its orange tile roofs, is worth mentioning. Besides its advantageous location on one of the best beaches on Baie Nettlé, it offers a whole range of services and facilities to ensure its guests an enjoyable stay, including two pools, hot-tubs and tennis courts. It also has flawlessly comfortable rooms of generous proportions.

Long Bay

La Samanna
US$715 bkfst incl.
≈, ℜ;
B.P. 4077, Long Bay
☎05.90.87.64.00
⇄05.90.87.87.86
If a dream hotel exists, it could very well be La Samanna, built at the top of a cliff, near one the best beaches on the island, Long Bay. Its design takes full advantage of the unbeatable location. The restaurant, rooms and lobby face the sparkling waves, and no

matter where you look the view is beautiful. Special attention has been taken with the decor: for example, the lobby is adorned with a small ceramic-tile fountain, while the walls are covered with Middle Eastern tapestries, lending the area a particular charm. The comfortable rooms are also tastefully decorated.

Grand Case

The pretty town of Grand Case has a good choice of accommodations sure to please, whether you're looking for budget-class hotels or luxury resorts.

Hévea
420 F
163 Boul. Grand Case, 95170
☎05.90.87.56.85
⇄05.90.87.83.88
A few reasonably priced places, by Saint-Martin standards, are located in the centre of town. Among these, the Hévea, set up in a sweet little house, is worth a look. The rooms are far from luxurious, but are decorated with special attention, with wooden beams and antique furniture that lend them a singular charm. This small hotel has two rooms and six studios (three of which are air-conditioned). Good value for your money, but be forewarned that reservations are not always respected.

Grand Case Beach Motel
450 F
K
97150
☎05.90.87.87.75
⇄05.90.87.26.55
Postal address: B.P. 175 Philipsburg, Sint Maarten
The Grand Case Beach Motel also offers reasonably priced rooms, which offer a basic level of comfort, and have the distinct advantage of including an equipped kitchenette. The decor is disappointing, but at least the rooms have a view of the sea.

Les Alizés
450 F
10 Allée des Escargots, 97150
☎05.90.87.95.38
⇄05.90.29.31.71
Inexpensive accommodation is available at Les Alizés motel. There is nothing luxurious about the place; the rooms all offer rudimentary comfort (the bare minimum) and have a modest decor, but the establishment is located conveniently close to the beach.

Pavillon
950 F bkfst incl., studio
≡, *K*
97150
☎05.90.87.96.46
⇄05.90.87.71.04
Right next door, the Pavillon also rents out

rooms equipped with kitchenettes and beautiful terraces opening out on the waves. Its decor sports brighter, more tropical colours, and the rooms have rattan furniture in pastel shades. The place is very well maintained.

Grand Case Beach Club
1,100 F
≈, ≡, *K*
97150
☎05.90.87.51.87
⇄05.90.87.59.93
At the very end of Grand Case Beach stands the long, white, one-storey Grand Case Beach Club. A tad old-fashioned, it comprises no fewer than 72 rooms, which are large and offer all modern conveniences as well as a balcony overlooking the beach. There is also access to another beach. A small, attractively laid-out garden borders the beach, where a host of water activities is organized. The establishment is a few minutes' walk from the village; guests can therefore easily enjoy the advantages of Grand Case while basking in peaceful surroundings.

Atlantide
1,200 F
K, ≡
B.P. 5140, 97150
☎05.90.87.09.80
⇄05.90.87.12.36
The Atlantide hotel was built just outside the centre of Grand Case, so guests are near the action, but still enjoy a quiet setting with direct access to the beach. Each prettily decorated, well-maintained room has a terrace looking out over the water so you can appreciate those beautiful seascapes. The reception is very friendly.

Petit Hôtel
1,820 F
≡, *K*
97150
☎05.90.29.09.65
⇄05.90.87.09.19
A lovely white residence, elegantly adorned with ceramic tiles, houses the Petit Hôtel, a magnificent lodging that may not be luxurious, but is nevertheless quite comfortable. Guests stay in large, thoroughly comfortable rooms, charmingly decorated with woodwork. Though the establishment does not have the convenience of being right downtown (it is a short distance away), it has the advantage of being right by the ocean.

Esplanade Caraïbe
2,080 F
≈, ≡, *K*, ⊗
B.P. 5007, 97150
☎*05.90.87.06.55*
⇄*05.90.87.29.15*
You can't miss the Esplanade Caraïbe's buildings, built on a hillside overlooking the bay of Grand Case. They are visible from town. Everything here ensures the guests' comfort: the kitchenette is particularly well equipped, the studio sitting-rooms are spacious, the rooms are attractively decorated with beautiful woodwork (doorway, ceiling and staircase for the suites with mezzanine) and they offer sea views.

Anse Marcel

No doubt attracted by the beauty of the location and the superb beach, several resorts have been built around the little cove of Anse Marcel.

Hôtel Privilège
1,700 F, bkfst incl.
≡
97056
☎*05.90.87.37.37*
⇄*05.90.87.33.75*
http://hotelprivilege.free.fr
The Hôtel Privilège occupies a small section of Anse Marcel, back a bit from the beach. It is set up inside a quaint wooden building of typical Caribbean charm. The ground floor of the building houses a row of shops. The airy rooms, located upstairs, are adorned with large windows looking out over the garden and are well furnished with colonial-style pieces that don't overwhelm. Hammocks are strung up on the balconies.

Panoramic Privilege
1,884 F + taxes, bkfst incl.
≈, ℜ, ≡
97150
☎*05.90.87.38.38*
⇄*05.90.87.44.12*
Upon arriving in Anse Marcel, you'll notice a road climbing up into the hills. At the summit is the Panoramic Privilege resort. It may not be right on the beach, but it does offer an exceptional view of Anse Marcel and a tranquil setting ideal for people looking for relaxation. The rooms have balconies from which to contemplate the sea, and tennis courts and a spa are available for the use of guests. The complex also comprises the **Horizon** hotel, which has attractive, cheerfully coloured rooms, all equipped with large bathrooms.

Caye Blanche
1,900 F
≈, ≡, *K*
97150
☎*05.90.87.30.30*
⇄*05.90.87.48.55*
Caye Blanche has opted for a decor that is unique in

Saint-Martin: it manages to imbue the rooms with a soothing quality and keeps guests cool no matter what time of day. This is achieved with a pinkish-tiled floor, white walls and sofas and a few pieces of wooden furniture. The bathrooms feature pretty, coloured tiles, which are a pleasant addition and complement the simple, refined decor of this establishment, one of the loveliest in Saint-Martin. The entire hotel is flawlessly elegant; the terraces, appointed with teak furniture, overlook the pool and quiet garden. Some rooms are equipped with kitchenettes, and a cook is available upon request.

Le Méridien
ℜ, ≡, ≈
B.P. 581,
97056
☎05.90.87.67.00
⇄05.90.87.30.38
Le Méridien, a large resort containing **L'Habitation Lonvilliers** *(1,280 F)* and **Le Domaine** *(1,610 F)*, occupies almost all of Anse Marcel. A vast garden with a profusion of flowering plants, ideal for a stroll, surrounds these buildings, and the whole setup is surrounded by the beach and the sea. L'Habitation de Lonvilliers has very beautiful rooms. Recently built right next door, Le Domaine offers equally comfortable rooms. A bamboo-lined lane leads the way. It goes without saying that the setting is superb and very peaceful.

Cul-de-Sac

Belvedere Residence
2,400 F/week
97150
☎05.90.87.37.89
⇄05.90.87.30.52
Compared to the other beaches on the island, the Baie de French Cul-de-Sac is under-developed. There are, however, a few hotels, including the Belvedere Residence on a hillside in an unfortunately dull setting. The rooms are comfortable but only somewhat make up for this drawback. Guests have the use of a big pool.

Anchorage Little Key Hotel
1,900 F, bkfst incl.
≡, ≈, ℜ
French Cul-de-Sac, 97150
☎05.90.29.55.55
⇄05.90.87.49.23
www.little-key.com
Another hotel complex has been built in this part of the island: the Anchorage Little Key Hotel, which is actually a nicer property. Buildings harbouring its attractively decorated rooms and two- to three-room bungalows are set amid its expansive landscaped grounds. The place is extremely pleasant, as it has been arranged so that many rooms have a view overlooking the

French Cul-de-Sac, while others overlook the garden.

Mont Vernon

Jardins de Chevrisse
750 F studio, 920 F villa
≡, *K*
97150
☎05.90.87.37.79
⇄05.90.87.38.03
The Jardins de Chevrisse comprises several yellow-walled, orange-roofed cottages, built in close proximity to each other. These close quarters are certainly not conducive to intimacy, but the rooms are quite acceptable. A profusion of plants makes the rooms and their terraces somewhat more private.

Orient Bay Hotel
750 F + 5% for a studio
980 F + 5% for a villa
≈, ≡, *K*
Mont Vernon 1, Route Cul-de-Sac, 97150
☎05.90.97.31.10
⇄05.90.87.37.66
The profusion of flowering oleanders and red hibiscus is a pleasant surprise upon entering the grounds of the Orient Bay Hotel and makes up for the lack of a garden. The blaze of colour also brightens up the pale pink villas. These are located in an area set back from the beach, but a nice pool makes up for this.

Alizea
1,080 F, bkfst. incl.
≈, ℜ, ≡, *K*
25 Mont Vernon
☎05.90.87.33.42
⇄05.90.87.41.15
A lovely path lined with bouganvillea and bay-trees leads to the Alizea hotel. Although it is a bit far from the beach, it offers a spectacular view from its location above the shimmering waves. Guests enjoy comfortable studios with equipped kitchenettes in a pleasant setting.

Mont Vernon
1,500 F
≈, ≡, ℜ
B.P. 1174, 97062
☎05.90.87.62.00
⇄05.90.87.37.27
The Mont Vernon hotel stands at the foot of the hill of the same name, which lies at the northern tip of Orient Bay. Standing five storeys tall, the buildings, fitted out with blue, green or pink balconies, house large rooms, decorated with rattan furniture in the same colours. Guests also benefit from a vast, pleasant garden, which extends to Orient Bay's magnificent beach.

Orient Bay

Skirting the ribbon of fine sand that trims superb Orient Bay, on spacious, well laid-out grounds, is a row of hotel complexes built to cater to guests seeking out one of the prettiest spots on the island. Most of the establishments are comfortable, actually luxurious, and benefit from a lovely garden and direct beach access.

Club Orient
990 F
ℜ, *K*
97150
☎ ***05.90.87.33.85***
⇄ ***05.90.87.33.76***
Club Orient is Saint-Martin's one and only clothing-optional resort. It consists of a series of clapboard cottages, scattered over extensive seaside grounds, brightened up here and there by a palm tree or a few bushes. Guests enjoy unfettered comfort; indeed, this peaceful and secluded site is a true little paradise. However, the beach and the facilities are not reserved exclusively for naturists, and are open to all.

La Plantation
1,040 F studio
1,450 F for a suite, bkfst incl.
K, ≈, ≡
97150
☎ ***05.90.29.58.00***
⇄ ***05.90.29.58.08***
La Plantation hotel is a series of pretty Creole-style cottages done up in warm colours. The rooms, with their pretty colours and bamboo and rattan furniture, fit in perfectly with the environment. The hotel is a little way from the beach but the grounds have a well-kept garden, where a profusion of flowered plants provides a buffer between other hotel properties.

Hoste
1,110 F garden view
1,200 F sea view
≈ ≡
97150
☎ ***05.90.87.42.08***
⇄ ***05.90.87.39.96***
With a mere 28 rooms, Hoste combines the intimacy of a small hotel with the comfort of larger establishments. Its charming pastel-coloured bungalows have a lovely view of the bay and house simply decorated but comfortable rooms. Moreover, guests will be treated to friendly and attentive service.

St. Tropez
1,200 F
≈, ≡
☎ ***05.90.87.42.01***
⇄ ***05.90.87.41.69***
The St. Tropez, which includes the Boca Raton, Capri and Palm Beach hotels, is located on a small plot of land, of which it makes judicious use. Several buildings have been built in different styles, housing 84 pleasantly decorated suites. Though we could fault the tiny garden, the place is well located, with access to the beach.

Palm Court
1,280 F
≡ ≈, *K*
☎05.90.87.42.01
This small hotel with kitchenette-equipped rooms is a good address to keep in mind for those who don't want to eat all their meals in restaurants. First and foremost, the rooms are functional: the kitchenette has a microwave and the room has both a dining area and a living room area. The bathrooms are spacious, the decor is simple but pleasant and there is a balcony overlooking the small garden.

Esmerelda
1,500 F, 2,200 F sea view
≈, ≡, ℜ
97071
☎05.90.87.36.36
⇄05.90.61.05.44
The superb Esmeralda complex consists of several luxurious villas in a vast garden graced with an abundance of plants and flowers. Each of the bungalows, at a fair distance from each other, have only a few rooms and each offers guests the luxury of a virtually private pool. The rooms, charmingly adorned with rattan furniture, warm colours and flowers, are another good reason to opt for this establishment.

Green Cay Village
2,340 F
≈, ≡, ℜ, *K*
B.P. 3006, 97064
☎05.90.87.38.63
⇄05.90.87.39.27
Not far from the Orient Bay Hotel is the luxurious Green Cay Village. The goal here is to satisfy guests looking for peace and quiet. Accordingly, the rooms are not crammed into large buildings, but rather guests stay in charming, beautifully decorated little houses, each with a private pool and a lovely terrace offering a view of the sea.

Restaurants

Marigot

Wonderful meals complemented by a view of either Baie de Marigot or the marina can be enjoyed at several spots around town.

Delices de France
$
Rue Général de Gaulle
Sandwiches and pastries are easy to find for lunch or breakfast. Delices de France sells delicious croissants and *pains au chocolat* (chocolate croissants) early in the morning. The lunchtime menu (around 50 F) is very

simple, made up essentially of quiches and sandwiches.

Boulangerie-Pâtisserie
$
If you happen to walk along Rue de la Liberté, next to the courthouse, you'll see a bakery and pastry shop that also serves sandwiches and salads. It has an attractive terrace that is popular at noon, even though it's right on the street.

Bar de la Mer
$$-$$$
1 Rue de la Liberté
☎05.90.87.81.79
Bar de la Mer is definitely one of the city's institutions. Known for its friendly, relaxed atmosphere, it has a bay-side terrace and a menu that fits in perfectly with its environment. Dishes, like salads, hamburgers, fish and seafood, are simple but good. Outdoor barbecue evenings are particularly popular: the cook prepares tender steaks and fish, filling the air with irresistible aromas.

The marina also attracts crowds of people. It is a pleasant spot with many restaurants offering simple menus (grilled fish, salad). They are located one next to the other, and each has a cozy terrace with a view of the marina.

Belle Époque
$$-$$$
☎05.90.87.70.70
Belle Époque, both an early riser and a night owl, serves breakfast as well as pizza, salad and pasta. The place is pleasant enough to make you forget that the fruit in the salad is canned! Nevertheless, the meals are good.

Brasserie de la Gare
$$-$$$
☎05.90.87.20.64
Quite possibly among the nicest restaurants in the area, the Brasserie de la Gare has a large dining room that opens onto a large terrace and the marina. Here, it goes without saying that the ambiance is relaxed and the space crowded. Also, the menu is varied enough to please all tastes and budgets, including grilled meats, salads, fish and spiny lobster.

Le Saint-Germain
$$-$$$
☎05.90.87.92.87
At one end of the marina is the Saint-Germain, where you can savour delicious meal or dessert crepes. The dining room, with large picture windows, looks out over the entrance to the marina. Also open for breakfast.

Chanteclair
$$$
☎05.90.87.94.60
Next door, the Chantelclair is also right on the marina. The choice of dishes, each more succulent than the last, is extensive. A few tasty examples are the *thon grillé avec légumes au vinaigre balsamique* (grilled tuna with vegetables in balsamic vinegar) or the *coquilles Saint-Jacques bardées de magret*. If you're in the mood for Creole specialties, you can opt for the Caribbean menu, which includes *accras*, grilled red snapper and coconut pie.

Mini-Club
$$$
Rue de la Liberté
☎05.90.87.50.69
Mini-Club is Marigot's oldest restaurant and, year after year, its cuisine never disappoints. Whether you're in the mood for fish, stuffed crab or some kind of Creole specialty, this is the place to go in the city. Moreover, the place has a pleasant location right on the bay.

Charolais
$$$$
Rue Félix Éboué, corner G. de Gaulle
☎05.90.87.93.19
The Charolais is located in the centre of town, away from the sea. The beach feels far away here, since the decor is more along the lines of an American ranch, with wooden walls decorated with troughs, pitchforks and cattle-breeding tools. This decor was chosen in accordance with the house specialty: beef, always top quality and always served in generous portions.

La Vie en Rose
$$$$
Boulevard de France
☎05.90.87.54.42
Housed in a magnificent colonial home, La Vie en Rose unquestionably ranks among the city's best restaurants. The restaurant is made up of two parts, a terrace opening out onto the street and an upstairs dining room. During the day, patrons dine on the terrace, which is fitted out with parasols and benefits from the port's lively atmosphere. The meals are honestly prepared but the service tends to be somewhat brusque. For a more stylish evening meal opt for the dining room, which is topped off with a magnificent coffered ceiling. The dishes are very refined and the meals presented as a series of delicious dishes

and little details. The service is also more courteous.

Friar's Bay (Baie des Pères)

Friar's Bay Beach Café
$-$$
This beachfront café, where you can enjoy your meal right on the sand, is hard to miss. Served here are good, simple dishes, such as smoked chicken, salads and burgers, perfect for lunch if you do not wish to stray from the beach.

Sandy Ground

Marios Bistrot
$$$-$$$$
Marios Bistrot stands on the edge of the arm of the sea that links the Caribbean Sea to Simson Bay Lagoon, and its dining room pleasantly overhangs the water. The restaurant also has a lovely decor, composed of sky-blue walls, ceramic tiles and beautiful lamps. An inviting ambiance radiates from this room, which is perfect for romantic dinners. The menu will also satisfy you, as it offers refined dishes such as *poêlée de coquilles Saint-Jacques au risotto à la crème de crabe* or *panequet de saumon*, always succulently prepared. Guests must also make a point of saving room for dessert, as the menu offers so many sublime goodies.

Baie Nettlé

Chez Swan
$
For a change from the buffet formula typical of large hotels in this area, you can have breakfast at Chez Swan, located in the Baie Nettlé shopping centre.

Ma Ti Beach
$$-$$$
☎05.90.87.01.30
There is another option when you neither want to leave Baie Nettlé nor submit yourself to another buffet: Ma Ti Beach. This restaurant has a large dining room and a large terrace set up directly on the beach. The ambiance is pleasant and the meals, though nothing extraordinary, are adequate.

Long Bay

You are sure to spend an unforgettable evening—one that will please your stomach as well as your wallet—at the La Samanna hotel's (see p 95) restaurant ***($$$$)***. It has two dining rooms: the one next to the bar, with parasols, is perfect during the day, while the other, a magnificent dining room, offering an unobstructed view of the ocean and an elegant yet relaxed atmosphere. The menu varies according to what is available, but the dishes, artfully concocted and made from the freshest products on the market, are always a real treat.

Grand Case

Charming little Grand Case has a surprising number of good restaurants along its main street. The biggest challenge is to choose from amongst the menus, each of which is more appetizing than the last.

Coin des Amis
$-$$
If you like authenticity, you simply have to eat a grilled fish from one of the waterfront stands, like Coin des Amis. Saint-Martin locals arrive at their weather-beaten wooden shacks in the early morning to begin preparing grilled fish and crab on make-shift barbecues. Despite these meagre facilities they concoct some divine little morsels.

Michael's Café
$-$$
Right on the edge of the beach, Michael's Café is another friendly place in Grand Case for breakfast or lunch. Sandwiches and hamburgers are among the noontime offerings.

California
$$
For a delicious pizza by the ocean, head to California. If you prefer to eat in your room, keep in mind that this restaurant prepares food to go.

L'Amandier
$$-$$$
28 Boulevard de Grand Case
☎05.90.87.24.33
A few tables and chairs and some parasols planted here and there form the basis of the decor of this pleasant, unpretentious seaside restaurant. L'Amandier is primarily a family restaurant, primarily because of the pool, which children adore. Comfortably seated beneath a parasol, a refreshment in their hands, parents can watch their offspring, who play to their heart's delight! A good place for an afternoon meal.

Restaurant du Soleil
$$-$$$
☎05.90.87.92.32
For a good lunch that doesn't break the bank, head to the Restaurant du Soleil, which offers a decent bite to eat. Patrons here can enjoy simple dishes, like a Niçoise salad or a more exotic salad (large prawns and pineapple), quiche Lorraine or an omelette while comfortably seated in a lovely blue-and-yellow dining room, beyond which the sea stretches out into the distance.

Rainbow
$$$-$$$$
One of Grand Case's fine restaurants, Rainbow is advantageously situated right by the ocean. Guests will savour fish and seafood dishes in a lovely dining room with a simple and sparse decor, essentially adorned with flowering plants. Among the specialties, you can try the mahi-mahi in Creole sauce or the *poêlée de gambas* (pan-fried prawns), exquisitely served. The atmosphere is peaceful and service is courteous.

Chez Martine
$$$-$$$$
☎05.90.87.51.59
The main street in Grande Case is lined by one good restaurant after another, one of which is Chez Martine. This restaurant offers its patrons a lovely dining room that opens out onto the sea and a menu that presents, day after day, the classics of French cuisine.

Le Cottage
$$$-$$$$
97 Boulevard de Grand Case
☎05.90.29.03.30
Le Cottage, one of the best restaurants on the island, is also on the main street. This welcoming restaurant, with a lovely terrace and an attractive interior, offers a fabulous experience for all the senses. Its French cuisine, particularly tasty and innovative, is lovingly presented. Le Cottage is also distinguished by its excellent wine list. A sommelier, passionate about his work, is pleased to propose a wine glass or a bottle of wine to accompany your meal. Furthermore, the quality and kindness of the service are notable here. Don't hesitate to end your meal with a desert: they're succulent.

Fish Pot
$$$$
☎05.90.87.50.88
The Fish Pot has a well-established reputation and is always spoken of with a sigh of satisfaction. The reason for this is quite simple: it is one of those places where the lobster, red snapper, shrimp and other bounties from the sea are always fresh and divinely prepared. This restaurant has earned its high standing and, though not stuffy, ranks among the city's most elegant restaurants.

Le Pressoir
$$$$
☎05.90.87.76.62
A completely renovated Creole house harbours one of the best restaurants in town, Le Pressoir, whose menu heralds the feast awaiting you within. Whether you opt for the house green salad or the fish soup with rouille, your meal will start off with a flourish. The equally deli-

cious main courses include such delectable dishes as lobster navarin with herb sauce and salmon with puréed asparagus. Finally, the menu would hardly be complete without offering a decadent treat for dessert, including *gratin de fruits rouges*, made with red berries and currants, and a chocolate dessert with pear sauce. The service is courteous and you are sure to pass a pleasant evening here.

Le Tastevin
$$$$
☎05.90.87.55.47
Just a few steps beyond you'll come upon another restaurant with an equally delightful menu—Le Tastevin. All of the dishes are delicious, including the *daurade de saumon aux agrumes* (salmon with citrus fruits). The 340 F set menu is another possibility, offering an enticing choice of dishes, each accompanied by a glass of astutely chosen wine.

Anse Marcel

Cotonier
$$$
☎05.90.87.44.56
Just before the road leading to Anse Marcel, there is a Creole cottage that houses Cotonier, a restaurant that concocts dishes marrying the flavours of the Caribbean with the fragrance of Provence. There are always innovative specialties to taste.

Le Barbecue
$$-$$$
Hôtel Méridien
It's hard to miss the Méridien hotel in Anse Marcel, as it occupies nearly the entire site. The place is lovely and overlooks a vast crescent of blond sand. Many clients come here for a meal, even if they aren't staying here. It's good to know that at lunch time, the restaurant offers an honest menu. Its reasonably priced dishes (including hamburgers and salads) are simple, but delicious and portions are generous. What's more, service is kind. During the evening, the hotel offers another option, **Belle France *($$$$)*,** which specializes in more refined—and more expensive—French cuisine.

La Calypso
$$
In addition to the Méridien hotel's buildings, Anse Marcel has a lovely shopping area that is home to some lovely boutiques as well as some restaurants. Among them is La Calypso, which introduces you to the flavours of Creole cuisine.

La Louisiane
$$-$$$
La Louisiane is another restaurant that offers a varied

menu featuring tasty dishes, notably some lovely salads, crepes and pizza. You can also try more elaborate items based on fish or meat. Besides good food, the restaurant features a pleasant, simple decor and a friendly ambiance. The place is just as enticing at lunchtime, when the menu features reasonably priced daily specials, as it is in the evening, when you can select a meal of several courses.

Mont Vernon

Taitu
$$
The Taitu is a good spot to keep in mind for lunch, when you can enjoy an omelette, a sandwich or some Creole specialty while comfortably seated on the terrace surrounded by lush greenery.

Mont Vernon
$$-$$$
The restaurant on the premises of the hotel Mont Vernon has two dining rooms, one in an interior courtyard where each table boasts a lovely blue beach umbrella, and the other inside, attractively adorned with rattan furniture. In a convivial atmosphere, guests can savour various dishes ranging from Creole *accras* to hamburgers, not to mention a wonderful selection of fish and meat dishes.

Orient Bay

You won't find any fancy restaurants on the shores of Orient Bay, but there is a good selection of seaside restaurants serving simple and varied fare from pizza to hamburgers, not to mention sandwiches, salads and Mexican food. People tend to stop by between swims, and a friendly and relaxed atmosphere prevails.

Among these restaurants, the **Bikini Beach *($$-$$$)*** stands out because of its large dining room, which opens out on the beach, and its festive atmosphere. The menu offers meals that are hardly extravagant and a little pricey, but they make good lunch fare.

Waikiki
$$-$$$
The Waikiki is another fairly charming beachside restaurant. Its menu is more elaborate than that of Bikini Beach, and the food is good, but somewhat expensive.

Booboo Jam
$$
Other restaurants on the beach at Oriental Bay attract their clientele with live music featuring local musicians. Among them is

Booboo Jam, which stands out for its particularly relaxed atmosphere. Performances are generally held Sunday afternoons. Any time of day, simple meals like pizza, hamburgers, sandwiches or salads can be had.

Entertainment

The sun sets early over St. Martin, around 7pm; and it gets very dark. This doesn't mean the island has no nightlife, though—quite the contrary, in fact! Discotheques, bars and casinos start welcoming revellers in the late afternoon, when seaside spots offer drinks complemented by the spectacle of the setting sun. The excitement reaches its pinnacle during Carnival time.

Bars and Nightclubs

Marigot

Bar de la Mer
port of Marigot
The Bar de la Mer has a pretty terrace with a view of the sea. People come to enjoy the relaxed atmosphere and chat with friends.

Those who prefer to end the evening at the marina go to the terrace at the Brasserie de la Gare, where an unpretentious atmosphere reigns.

To end the night on a lively note and dance to your heart's content, you can check out one of two dance clubs that have made a name for themselves; **Club One** *(Marina la Royale, ☎05.90.87.98.41)* and **Privé** *(at the city's west entrance, Rue de la Liberté, ☎05.90.87.95.77)*, which has a great terrace.

Baie Nettlé, Long Bay and Anse Marcel

Several popular locales near the tourist villages are known for their lively atmosphere or as great spots to pass the night away.

The large resorts, be it the Méridien (Anse Marcel), the Flamboyant (Baie Nettlé), the Mercure Simson (Baie Nettlé) or La Samanna (Long Bay), all have lovely bars offering magnificent ocean views.

On the hills overlooking Anse Marcel is the **Privilège Resort** hotel, which, aside from a magnificent view, has a lively piano bar.

Friar's Bay (Baie des Pères)

Musicians are often invited to play on the banks of Friar's Bay on Sundays, creating a festive ambiance that reigns throughout the afternoon.

Grand Case

Coco Club *(boulevard de Grand Case)* is the local bar. Its large premises open onto the street, where you can have a drink or an ice cream. In the evening, the place livens up, and the atmosphere is pleasant.

Orient Bay

Several restaurants opening out on Orient Bay are great spots to while away your vacation with a late afternoon drink. On certain days, musicians come and play by the seaside. Two restaurants have won acclaim amongst local music lovers: Bikini Beach and Booboo Jam, where the laid-back atmosphere is very pleasant. Booboo jam is also known for its lively Friday nights.

Casinos

Though there are casinos only on the Dutch side of the island, no fewer than eight occupy the small territory of Sint Maarten (see p 138). Many of the hotels on the French side have free shuttle services for high-rolling guests looking to try their luck.

Shopping

The boutiques are numerous, the products countless; we have selected a few of the more interesting places, either because of the products they sell, or their prices.

Marigot

Clothing

Marigot is truly the centre of high fashion in Saint-Martin. By poking around a little, and if you're not averse to spending money, you'll be able to find a few of the great French and Italian designers' latest creations.

Les Gens de... *(Rue du Général de Gaulle)*, **Milano** *(Rue du Général de Gaulle)* and **Romana** *(Rue de la République)* are among the beautiful boutiques where you might just succumb to temptation.

Other shopkeepers have opted for clothing lines that

are more suitable for the Caribbean climate, of a simpler style, often made of cotton or linen. Several lovely boutiques have set up shop around the marina; you will thus be spoiled for choice among dresses, sarongs, skirts and tops, well suited to the tropical climate.

For great, brightly coloured T-shirts, head to **Comptoir des Îles** *(Rue de la Liberté)* or to **PEER** (Rue Général de Gaulle), where the styles are lovely and varied.

Parents seeking clothes for their children will find just what they're looking for at **Pomme** *(Rue de l'Anguille)*, which offers both French and American collections.

Those in search of a swimsuit in the latest style can find just what they're looking for at **Banana Moon** (marina), which carries some lovely ones. Drop by **Bleu Soleil** *(Boulevard de France)*, which carries a fine assortment of designs.

The **market** is held Wednesday and Saturday mornings, but several merchants set up shop here every day during tourist season to sell all types of clothes: swimsuits, sarongs, T-shirts, shorts, cotton pants, dresses—in short, everything to suit all tastes. Wonderful seashell, silver and coral jewellery, as well as curios and souvenirs of all kinds can also be found here.

Accessories

What can we say that hasn't already been said about **Lancel** *(Rue du Général de Gaulle)*, as well known for its leather bags as for its magnificent selection of accessories.

Belts, handbags, fun jewellery are just a few of the small treasures that appeal to everyone and can be found at **Vie Privée** *(near the marina)*.

Jewellery

Several boutiques in Saint-Martin sell an abundance of fabulous Cartier jewellery, Lalique or Daum crystal vases and high quality leather goods. Even if you don't plan on buying anything, a visit to one of these places is a real feast for the eyes. **Goldfinger** *(Port la Royale marina)*, **Carat** *(Rue de la République)*, **Cartier** *(Rue de la République)*, **La Romana** *(Rue de la République)* and **Little Switzerland** *(Rue de la République)* are among the best of them.

Other boutiques, like **Passions** *(Rue du Général de Gaulle)*, offer more affordable jewellery made of mother-of-pearl, seashells or silver.

You will find very cute, reasonably priced coral necklaces and bracelets at **Schéhérazade** *(Rue du Général de Gaulle)*. Some of the gold jewellery is more expensive.

Perfume and Cosmetics

Prices of beauty products and perfume are on a par with those in North America and Europe. There are therefore no real bargains to be had here. Nevertheless, you can head to **Lipstick** *(Rue du Président Kennedy and Rue de la République)* or **Beauty and Scents** *(Rue du Général de Gaulle)*.

Groceries

For groceries, be it sausages, frozen foods, cookies or any other food product, head to the **Match** supermarket *(on the road leading to Grand Case)*.

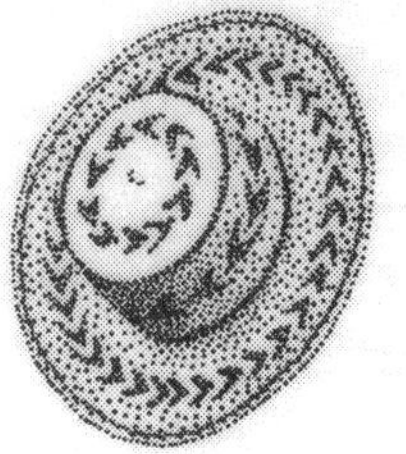

Wine and Spirits

For a stunning collection of vintage wines as well as more affordable bottles, you must check out **Goût du Vin** (*Rue de l'Anguille*), where you are sure to find something to satisfy your palate.

Souvenirs and Gifts

For more information on one of Saint-Martin's more renowned artists, make a stop at **Galerie de Roland Richardson** *(Rue de la République)*, where a few of this painter's works are exhibited and sold. The paintings of A. Minguet, exhibited at **Chez Minguet** *(Rue de la Liberté)*, also make lovely gifts. Antique furniture and *objets d'art* so lovely that few can resist await at **Mahogany**.

Creole arts and crafts, china and lace are among the little gifts to be found at **Paris Art et Cadeaux** *(Rue du Président Kennedy)*, **Primavera** *(Rue du Général de Gaulle)* and **Papagayo** *(Rue du Général de Gaulle)* boutiques.

Sporting Goods

For sporting goods of all sorts, **Team Number One** (*Rue du Palais de Justice*) is a good address to know in Marigot.

Fishing One (*rue Victor Maurasse*) is as well-known for its fishing gear as for its Arima and Top Sider boat shoes.

Stationery, Newspapers and Magazines

In addition to selling notebooks and pencils, **la Press** (*corner of Rue de la Liberté and Rue de l'Anguille*) is also a bookstore. Daily newspapers are available here as well as magazines.

Miscellaneous

Everything from baby bottles to beach articles, including towels and corkscrews, is available at **Forum Caraïbes** (*Rue St-James*) at reasonable prices.

Baie Nettlé

A small shopping centre has sprouted near Baie Nettlé's hotel complexes. In addition to two little restaurants serving breakfast, the mall comprises a well-stocked grocery store (wine, pastries, frozen food, cookies, chips) as well as a small shop where you can pick up **books, newspapers and magazines**.

Grand Case

Newspapers and Magazines

On Boulevard Grand Case, next to the Fish Pot, you can stock up on magazines and newspapers at **Paragraphe**.

Souvenirs and Gifts

Graffiti *(Boulevard de Grand Case)* is a little shop where painted statuettes, fun T-shirts, curios and a thousand and one Caribbean souvenirs are piled up higgledy-piggledy.

The delightful boutique **Sexy Fruits** *(Boulevard de Grand Case)* is the place to go if you're shopping for a straw hat, a T-shirt, silver jewellery or a *paréo*.

Groceries

Tony's *(Boulevard Grand Case, opposite the California restaurant)* grocery store is no supermarket, but can come in handy in a pinch for such essentials as water, cookies and other foodstuffs.

Slightly bigger, **Grand Case Superette** (facing the Coco Club) will definitely fill your basic needs.

For goods of higher quality, head to **Bounty** *(Boulevard Laurence)*, which is the city's fine foods market. Here, you'll find a large variety of foodstuffs and wines.

Anse Marcel

Clothing

A small shopping centre has been built around the Méridien's buildings. There are a great number of little boutiques with lovely collections of silk *paréos*, scarves of all sorts, an assortment of cotton dresses, and T-shirts.

Newspapers and Magazines

Among the boutiques in the shopping centre, there is a small stand where you can buy newspapers and magazines.

Souvenirs and Gifts

For red or blue coral jewellery, mother-of-pearl statuettes, or any other little treat, stop at **Schéhérazade**.

Sporting Gear

Water sports buffs are sure to appreciate **Budget Marine**, which sells all manner of accessories.

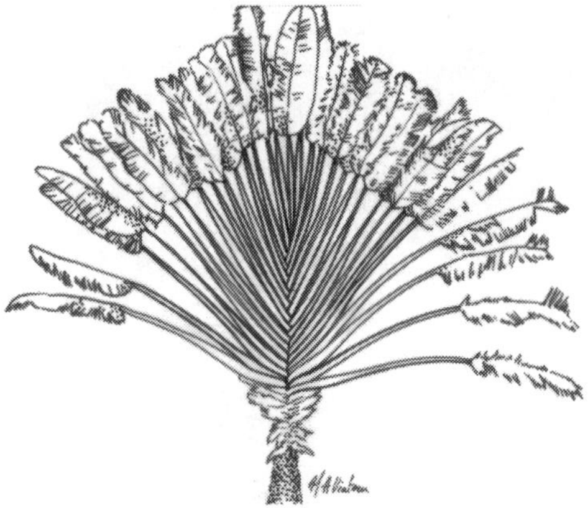

Sint Maarten

Salt is the root of Sint Maarten's history. The Arawaks had already named the island of St. Martin *sualouiga*, which means "land of salt," when this white substance, exploited because of the existence of salt marshes, first drew the attention of Dutch conquerors who settled in 1531.

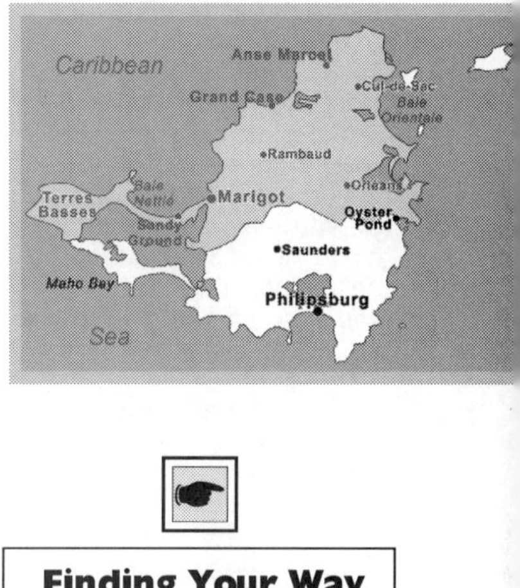

This labour-intensive industry was the source of the prosperity of the Dutch, who were the only ones to extract salt from Great Salt Pond until the 20th century. Philipsburg developed beside this salt-marsh and today luxurious shops assure work for many people in this great commercial city. The 1970s saw tourist towns like Mullet Bay and Oyster Pond come into their own. Thanks to magnificent beaches, they still enchant crowds of visitors who return year after year.

Finding Your Way Around

By Car

The 33km^2 of the Dutch part of the island are transected by very few roads. Most are in relatively good condition, although potholes here and there are an inconvenience. The most troublesome aspect of driving is the frequent deficiency, and occasional absence, of road signs, which makes it necessary to be very attentive.

From **Princess Juliana Airport**, there is only one road heading west. It passes the tourist village of **Mullet Bay**, leads to **Cupecoy**, and then enters the French portion of the island at **Terres Basses**.

To reach **Philipsburg** (10 km from the airport), take the same road eastward. The road forks just before the city; the right lane heads downtown, and the left circles **Great Salt Pond** and heads into the interior, toward the hamlets of **Madame Estate** and **Saunders**.

To reach **Dawn Beach** and **Oyster Pond**, follow the main road (the one toward Madame Estate) and take the respective turnoffs for these destinations.

Renting a Car

Princess Juliana Airport

Avis
☎***545-3959***

Budget
☎***545-4030***

Europcar
☎***544-2168***
⇄***544-2268***

Hertz
☎***545-4541***
⇄***545-4540***

Safari
☎***545-3180***

Sandyg
☎***545-3335***

Thrifty
☎***545-2393***
⇄***545-4231***

By Taxi

Reaching **Mullet Bay** and **Philipsburg** from the airport by taxi is simple, as there are plenty of cabs at the airport.

Airport:
the taxi stand is in front of the exit
☎***545-4317***

Philipsburg:
the taxi stand is on Front St., next to the pier
☎***542-2359***

By Bus

Buses travelling the main road are relatively frequent, and during the day it is not difficult to reach the **airport**, **Mullet Bay**, **Philipsburg**, **Marigot** or **Orient Bay**. It can be more difficult to reach smaller, isolated beaches.

Philipsburg:
bus stops are on Back St.

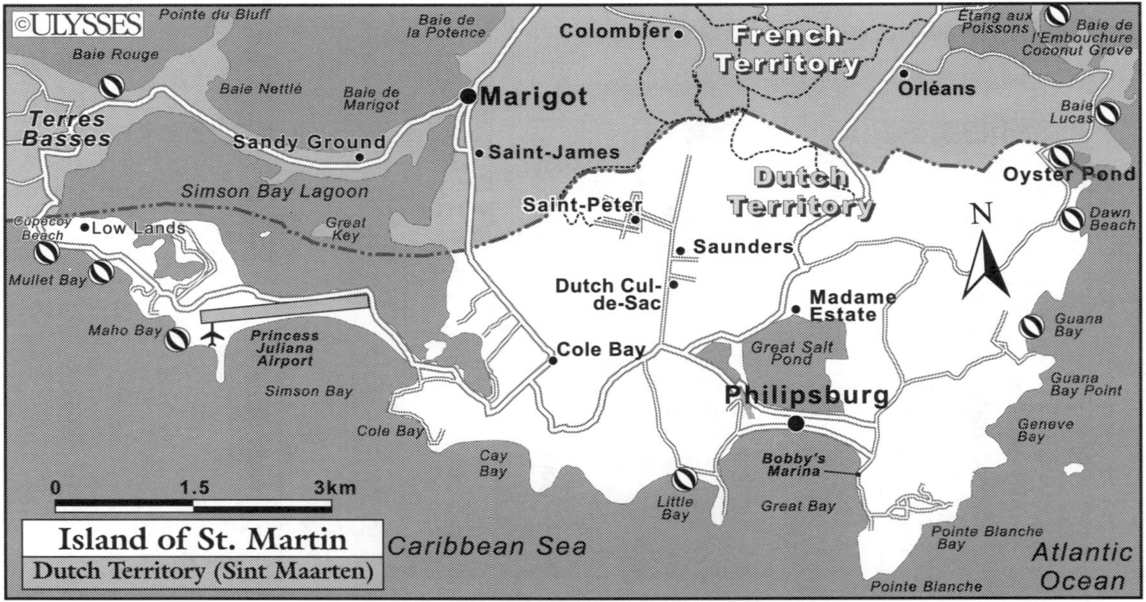
©ULYSSES
Pointe du Bluff
Baie de
la Potence
Colombier
French
Territory
Étang aux
Poissons
Baie de
l'Embouchure
Coconut Grove
Baie Rouge
Baie Nettlé
Baie de
Marigot
Marigot
Orléans
Baie
Lucas
Terres
Basses
Sandy Ground
Saint-James
Oyster Pond
Simson Bay Lagoon
Dutch
Territory
Saint-Peter
Cupecoy
Beach
Low Lands
Great
Key
Dawn
Beach
N
Saunders
Mullet Bay
Dutch Cul-
de-Sac
Madame
Estate
Maho Bay
Princess
Juliana
Airport
Cole Bay
Great Salt
Pond
Guana
Bay
Simson Bay
Philipsburg
Guana
Bay Point
Cole Bay
Geneve
Bay
Cay
Bay
Bobby's
Marina
0
1.5
3km
Little
Bay
Great Bay
Island of St. Martin
Dutch Territory (Sint Maarten)
Caribbean Sea
Pointe Blanche
Bay
Atlantic
Ocean
Pointe Blanche

Practical Information

Tourist Information

St. Maarten Tourist Bureau
23 Walter Nisbeth Rd.
3rd floor
Vineyard Office Park
Philipsburg
☎*542-2337*
⇄*542-2734*
www.st-maarten.com

Banks

Bank of Nova Scotia
Backstreet, Philipsburg
☎*542-4262*

Barclay's Bank
Front St., Philipsburg
☎*542-2567*

Chase Manhattan Bank
Philipsburg
☎*542-3801*

Post Office

Philipsburg:
Mon to Thu 7:30am to 5pm, Fri 7:30am to 4:30pm
at the corner of Vlaun and Richardson sts.
☎*542-2289*

Medical Care

Hospital:
Cay Hill
☎*543-1111*

Pharmacy:
Philipsburg
☎*542-2321*

Emergency:
☎*111*

Ambulance:
☎*130*

Central Drugstore:
Philipsburg
☎*542-2321*

Attractions and Beaches

In the Dutch part of the island, there is but one large city, Philipsburg, the heart of economic activity around which many residential neighbourhoods have grown. Philipsburg certainly is worth visiting, but it is not really the reason people travel to Sint Maarten. They are more attracted to the tourist enclaves, such as Oyster Pond and Mullet Bay, that have been built at the edges of superb beaches of golden sand.

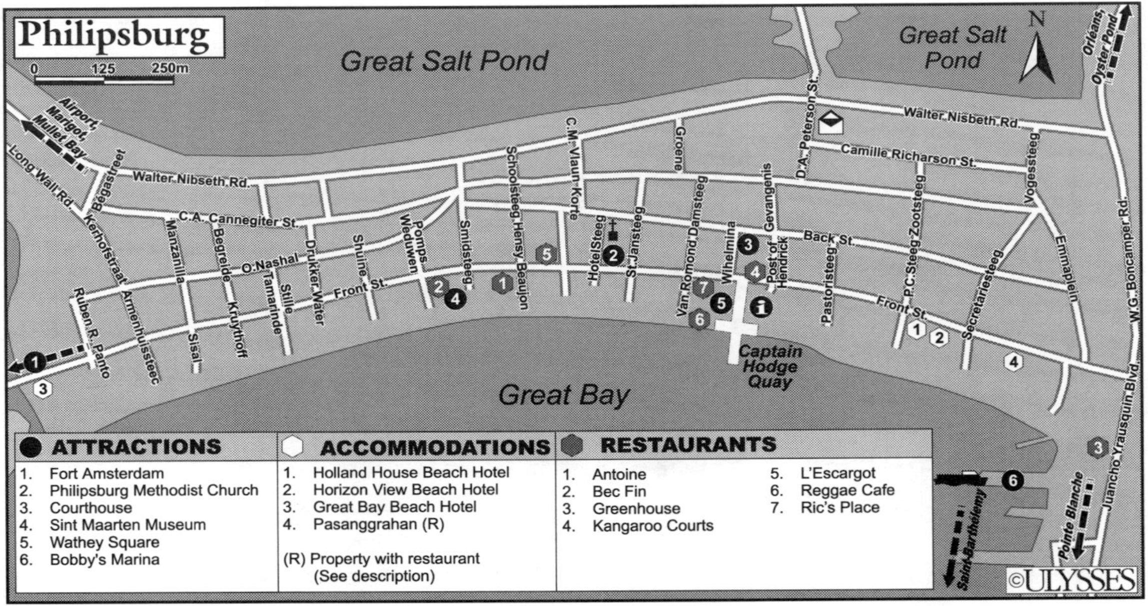
Philipsburg
0 125 250m
Great Salt Pond
Great Salt Pond
N
Orléans, Oyster Pond
Airport, Marigot, Mullet Bay
Long Wall Rd.
Begastreet
Walter Nisbeth Rd.
C.A. Cannegiter St.
Kerhofstraat
Manzanilla
Begreide
O.Nashal
Drukker Water
Shuine
Pomps Weduwen
Smidsteeg
Schoolsteeg Hensy Beaujon
C.M. Vlaun Korte
Groene
Hotel Steeg
St. Jansteeg
Van Romond Damsteeg
Wilhelmina
Post of Gevangenis
Hendrick
D.A. Peterson St.
Camille Richarson St.
Back St.
Pastoristeeg
P.C. Steeg Zootsteeg
Secretariesteeg
Vogessteeg
Emmaplein
W.G. Boncamper Rd.
Juancho Yrausquin Blvd.
Front St.
Ruben R. Panto
Armenhuissteec
Sisal
Kruythoff
Tamarinde
Stille
Captain Hodge Quay
Great Bay
Pointe Blanche
Saint-Barthélemy
ATTRACTIONS
1. Fort Amsterdam
2. Philipsburg Methodist Church
3. Courthouse
4. Sint Maarten Museum
5. Wathey Square
6. Bobby's Marina
ACCOMMODATIONS
1. Holland House Beach Hotel
2. Horizon View Beach Hotel
3. Great Bay Beach Hotel
4. Pasanggrahan (R)
(R) Property with restaurant (See description)
RESTAURANTS
1. Antoine
2. Bec Fin
3. Greenhouse
4. Kangaroo Courts
5. L'Escargot
6. Reggae Cafe
7. Ric's Place
©ULYSSES

Philipsburg

Philipsburg ★ was built on a thin strip of land bordered by Great Bay on one side and a vast salt marsh, Great Salt Pond, on the other. It was founded in 1763 by Commander John Philips. Much before this date, however, in 1631, the Dutch had established themselves here, in order to exploit this advantageous site (and the immense salt deposits of Great Salt Pond). To protect the first colonists, **Fort Amsterdam ★** was erected at the eastern tip of the bay, at Little Bay.

Philipsburg Methodist Church

This fort did not resist attack long; Spanish soldiers conquered it only two years later, and a large garrison charged with protecting the Spanish fleet set up camp. Bit by bit, this strategic choice proved less judicious, and in 1648 the Spanish abandoned St. Martin, leaving a destroyed fort in their wake. That same year, the Dutch claimed a part of the island. The fort was rebuilt shortly thereafter and protected the territory until the 19th century. The ruins of Fort Amsterdam are now open to the public and if you visit them you will also be treated to a magnificent view of the city.

From morning to night, bustling Philipsburg is overrun by fervent crowds of visitors disembarking from cruise ships anchored in the bay or arriving from the nearby tourist villages. They come to shop in the city's boutiques, which offer an incredible variety of goods. Clustered mostly along Front Street, the boutiques are lined up one after the other, with no shortage of sales and each offering a better deal than the last, to keep the shoppers coming. For some, the powerful noonday sun makes Philipsburg unbearable, while others thrive on the hustle and bustle.

Among this abundance of shop windows overflowing with gold jewellery, beauty products and liquor bottles, are some lovely, pastel-coloured cottages. Strolling along the street, **Philipsburg Methodist Church,** with a shingled facade, stands prettily between Hotelsteeg and St. Jansteeg streets.

A few steps away, facing the pier and Wathey Square, is a beautiful white building which houses the **Courthouse** ★. In 1792, the commander of Sint Maarten, Willem Hendrik Rink, ordered the construction of this building, since until then he had been governing from his own home, located at Cul-de-Sac, a great distance from Philipsburg. The architect John Handleigh was chosen to design it, and the next year, in 1793, the Courthouse was inaugurated. The stone walls enclose various rooms, including an office for the secretary of the governor as well as a few prison cells. The building was damaged by a hurricane in 1819 and it was not repaired until 1826, when a few modifications were made, including the addition of a small bell tower. Over the years, this building has served successively as a fire station, a prison, and finally a post office, and today it is very much a symbol of the island.

Finally, if you are interested in learning more about the Arawaks, the original inhabitants of the island, head to the **Sint Maarten Museum** *(US$2; Mon-Fri 10am to 4pm, Sat 10am to 2pm; 7 Front St., ☎542-4917),* located in a simple house right in the heart of the city. It exhibits some Arawak objects (three of which are original) that were discovered during excavations in the region of Mullet Bay, as well as some Dutch and Spanish items dating from the beginning of colonization, which were found at Fort Amsterdam.

Courthouse

After walking down Front St. with its innumerable shops, the **pier**, by **Wathey Square**, lapped by soothing waves, is a calming place to take advantage of a few minutes of relative tranquility.

Great Salt Pond, located north of Philipsburg, was exploited up until 1949. Most of the salt extracted was exported to the United States and the industry provided employment to a great many residents of St. Martin. The demise of the industry caused a serious crisis, and many people, finding themselves without income, were obliged to emigrate to other islands and more prosperous nations. Today, the marsh attracts a few curious visitors, but it is above all frequented by birds, notably herons.

In the easternmost part of the city is **Bobby's Marina**, crowded with boats that drop anchor here. Cruises to St. Barts also depart from here. The road then continues southward to **Pointe Blanche**, where there is a cluster of hotels and restaurants.

Outside of Philipsburg

Although it occupies a smaller territory, Sint Maarten is more populous than Saint-Martin, and most of its residents live on the outskirts of Philipsburg. The number of modest cottages that seem to be barely clinging to their foundations in these outlying neighbourhoods is surprising. Contrasting with the splendid homes along the coast, these houses are often the refuge of young and more or less legal workers who have migrated to the island in the hopes of earning a living.

The road that climbs the hills north of Philipsburg travels through **Dutch Cul De Sac** and **St. Peters**, where cottages stand one next to the other, seemingly arranged to occupy available space to its maximum potential. Essentially residential areas, these neighbourhoods offer little of interest to visitors.

After skirting Great Salt Pond, the main road leads to **Madame Estate**. This is the site of the **Sint Maarten Zoo** *(Mon to Fri 9am to 6pm, Sat and Sun 10am to 6pm; ☎22.748)*, where various species of animals from the Caribbean and South America can be observed. There is also a botanical garden here.

The Arawaks

Like the other islands of the Lesser Antilles, St. Martin was inhabited long ago by the Arawaks. These indigenous peoples lived in a hierarchical society and had their own myths and religious beliefs. They were quite skilled, and fashioned stone objects for the practice of their religion, several of which have been found in the Greater and Lesser Antilles. Some objects have also been found during excavations carried out under unusual conditions.

The relics on display at the museum were found in the 1960s during the pre-construction work for a hotel in Mullet Bay. The site foreman, having discovered a cave containing Arawak objects, alerted the Dutch authorities. The response was so long in coming that the foreman gave up waiting and instead of preserving the unique site, decided to use it as a septic tank. He may have saved some money, but at what price? Only three statuettes survived. Since then, other excavations have been carried out on St. Martin to learn more about the pre-Columbian peoples that lived on the island.

West of Philipsburg

The Simson Bay Lagoon begins about 5km west of Philipsburg; this is where most of the tourist activity on the Dutch side of the island takes place. The road is lined with comfortable hotels, some of which have been converted to "time-sharing" apartments, built near the airport and alongside beautiful beaches.

To reach the tourist village of Mullet Bay from Philipsburg or the airport, take the main road west.

Among these tourist locales is **Mullet Bay ★**. A town

consisting of a string of hotels, restaurants, casinos and boutiques, it is the centre of this part of the island. Guests of the surrounding hotels converge here to take advantage of the services and enjoy the holiday atmosphere and long sandy beaches (Maho Beach, Mullet Bay and Cupecoy Beach).

There are numerous resorts in this section of the island, and while the beaches here are not the jewels of the island, they do satisfy those craving fine sand and inviting surf. **Maho Beach** and **Mullet Beach**, both lined with hotels and condos, are often swarming and it can be difficult at times even to find enough space to spread out a towel. These are above all places to soak in the festive atmosphere and to see and be seen. Maho Bay also attracts Boeing 747–watchers because the airport is located at one end of the beach.

A little out of the way and offering a similar ambiance, **Cupecoy Beach** is a band of golden sand hidden at the foot of cliffs. A pleasant and popular spot, this is not a refuge for solitude-seekers.

East of Philipsburg

Continuing eastward past Philipsburg, the road penetrates the interior and passes through modest, ordinary-looking villages. Be attentive, though: along the road there are turnoffs for Guana Bay, Dawn Beach and Oyster Pond, where some attractive resorts as well as magnificent beaches are to be found.

Leaving Philipsburg, take the main road east. Barely a few kilometres out of the city, the road intersects a smaller road, which leads to Guana Bay.

Winding roads snake through the rolling hills of this region and modest wooden cottages gradually give way to lavish homes, a contrast that intensifies as you approach the ocean. **Guana Bay** is a pretty village of a few luxurious, sumptuous houses built on the hills overlooking blue-tinted waves. A little beach completes this inviting scene.

No road links Guana Bay and Dawn Beach directly. To reach Dawn Beach, backtrack to the main road, continue east and take the second turnoff toward the ocean.

An excellent road goes down the steep cliff and leads to a small public parking lot next to the magnificent **Dawn Beach** ★. You can settle down comfortably at one end of this lovely crescent of silky sand, where chairs and parasols can be rented. There is also a small bar-restaurant with long wooden tables for those who wish to take a break from their tanning session and quench their thirst.

You can reach Oyster Pond by water taxi from Dawn Beach for US$2.

Oyster Pond Bay ★★ has the particularity of being divided between France (Saint-Martin) and Holland (Sint Maarten), but passing from one side to the other is easy, since there is no border crossing. This pretty bay is developed on both sides.

On the way down the steep road to the beach, you'll notice that Oyster Pond Bay is almost entirely surrounded by hills, with only a narrow passage linking it to the Atlantic Ocean so that it looks like a small lake. This stretch of water is naturally quite calm and thus perfect for mooring boats, and there is a marina to accommodate them. A number of comfortable hotels accommodate the water-sports enthusiasts who frequent the spot.

Outdoor Activities

Scuba Diving and Snorkelling

Not far off the coast of Sint Maarten, there are coral reefs where snorkelers can thoroughly enjoy themselves. Most of the island's diving sites are located on the Dutch side, and the best-known spots are situated just off Dawn Beach and Maho Bay. Other sites are interesting, not for their coral but for their shipwrecks. Divers can go down to see the remains of the English vessel *HMS Proselyte*, which sank in 1801 off Great Bay, or the wreck of the tugboat in Mullet Bay. Schools of fish swim about in these decaying hulls.

Oceans Explorer
Simson Bay
☎*544-5252*
⇄*544-4357*

Dive Safari
Bobby's Marina, Philipsburg
☎*542-6024*

Sailing

The marina at Oyster Pond is the prime spot for watching beautiful sailboats rocking on the waves. If you'd like to do more than watch, there are some small private companies that offer sailing trips.

Hiking

Cole Bay Hill, a small mountain west of Philipsburg, is a pleasant climb. The hike takes about an hour and leads to the summit where an observation deck looks out on a splendid panorama. Bring water and plan the trip for the morning when the sun is not too hot.

Accommodations

Philipsburg

The Pasanggrahan Royal Guesthouse Hotel
US$105
ℜ, ⊗
Front St., P.O. Box 151
☎*542-3588*
⇄*542-2885*
This establishment is somewhat of an anomaly in Sint Maarten. Indeed, it has nothing in common with the ubiquitous modern high-rises, as the owners decided to opt for charm instead. The front lobby is set up in a lovely colonial-style residence, prettily adorned with antique furnishings, while the rooms themselves are housed in two beachfront buildings. The oldest of the two, also in the colonial style, comprises lovely rooms graced with attractive wooden shutters and rattan furniture. The second, newer building boasts a somewhat more modern decor and added comfort. In addition to its attractive layout, the hotel offers guests a friendly welcome, a waterfront restaurant and direct access to the beach. One small quibble: it is located on busy Front Street, although it is on one of the quieter

Creole houses on Saint Barts display fine architectural detail, such as this one with its wood trim. - *L.P.*

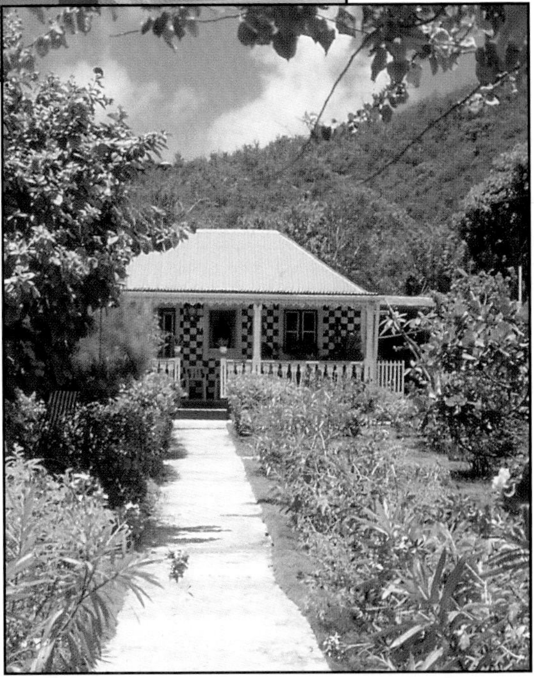

A pretty Creole house on Saint Barts urrounded by a magnificent garden. - *L.P.*

A lone sailboat moored ir Gustavia harbour, Saint Bart
- *Claude-Hervé Ba*

This fisherman's boat shows off its lovely blue and red colours on the waters at the port of Corossol.
- *L.P.*

stretches of this commercial thoroughfare.

Horizon View Beach Hotel
US$129
≡, ℜ, *K*
39 Front St.
☎543-2120
⇄542-0705

At the heart of the thriving city of Philipsburg, this hotel rents small, somewhat gloomy apartments. The most comfortable of them have a lovely view of the ocean. Though the hotel is located in the centre of the city's action, the rooms are quiet.

Holland House Beach Hotel
US$140
K
Front St.
☎542-2572
⇄542-4673
www.hhbh.com

A stone's throw from the Horizon View Beach Hotel stands the Holland House Beach Hotel, which also has a beachfront location. In the heart of the hustle and bustle of town, it doesn't exactly have an idyllic location. Nonetheless, it is tidy looking and a little more pleasant than its neighbour. The rooms are decent, too.

Great Bay Beach Hotel
US$220
ℜ, ≈, ≡, ⏲
Little Road Bay
☎542-2446
⇄542-2859
www.greatbayhotel.com

The charming, old-fashioned six-storey pastel-coloured buildings of the Great Bay Beach Hotel form a large complex on the outskirts of Philipsburg, located in a relatively quiet setting. Although the rooms are altogether decent and there is a pleasant sandy beach, the site itself is hardly enchanting.

Mullet Bay, Maho Beach and Cupecoy Beach

Boutiques, resorts, bars, restaurants and casinos make Mullet Bay and surroundings the busiest tourist spot on the island. This built-up region welcomes a large number of visitors who come to relax and have fun. There's just one problem: the main runway of the Princess Juliana Airport is right at the end of the beach, and the planes can be rather disruptive.

Over the last few years, several resorts in this tourist zone have been converted into comfortable apartment buildings whose units are rented out according to the time-share formula (see p 61). Such places will be referred to as "private clubs" so as to distinguish them from regular establishments. Even if you do not wish to become a member, you may still be able to stay in some such clubs, since their apartments are occasionally available for rent. A number of them go for about US$250 per night, but better deals are often to be had. Because they are private, we were unable to visit many of these establishments; thus can we only offer you a short description of the places in question.

Mary's Boon
US$175
⊗, ℜ, *K*
117 Simson Bay Rd.
☎545-4235
⇄545-3403
www.marysboon.com
Mary's Boon is visible as you disembark from the airplane, as it is located beside the runway. While this of course is a major disadvantage, the hotel offers 14 tastefully decorated rooms, some of which have a lovely balcony overlooking the beach. The rooms are all spacious and comfortable. Furthermore, particular attention is paid to service, which is always friendly.

The Atrium Resort
US$180
≡, ≈, ℜ
Pelican Rd.
☎544-2125
⇄544-2128
www.atrium-resort.com
This is one of the elegant resorts built on the shores of Simson Bay. Elegantly decorated, with fewer than 100 rooms, this is the perfect spot for peaceful relaxation. While the Atrium has no gym, its guests have access to the facilities of the Pelican Resort and Casino (see below).

Pelican Resort and Casino
US$200
≈, ℜ, ≡
P.O. Box 431
☎544-2503
⇄544-2133
www.pelicanresort.com
Located outside of this tourist town, near Philipsburg, this old-looking building, standing by the side of the road in a less than picturesque setting, does not look like much, but it does offer pleasant rooms.

Caravanserai Beach Resort
US$210
≡, ≈, ℜ
2 Beacon Hill Rd.
☎545-4000
⇄545-4001

www.caravan-sxm.com
This resort is set on spacious grounds, just a stone's throw from the landing strip at the Princess Juliana Airport. Beautifully set up, it is made up of a series of buildings atop small cliffs leading into the sea. But here, you'll spend your time contemplating the waves, because there is no beach; for a swim, guests have to go to nearby beaches. Nevertheless, the site is pleasant and the wooden buildings, right by the sea, are rather cute. The rooms themselves are located in motel-style buildings, but all of them are large and offer a sea view. There is a small shopping mall, a restaurant, a bar and a casino right on site.

Two hotels once formed the heart of the holiday village that is Maho Beach: these are the aptly named Maho Beach Hotel and the **Royal Islander Club** *($250; PO Box 2000, Philipsburg, ☎545-2388, ⇌545-3495)*. Although the latter has been converted into a private club, it is still possible to stay there. A multi-storey building that was built some years ago, it now looks somewhat outdated. It stands right on a lovely fine-sand beach.

Among the big hotels at the edge of this pretty white-sand bay rises the eight-storey **Maho Beach Hotel and Casino** *(US$325; ≈, ℜ, ≡; Maho Bay, ☎545-2115, ⇌545-3180, www.mahobeach.com)*. Every aspect of this hotel has been designed with the comfort of the guest in mind. Everything revolves around a huge pool in the centre of the complex: a bar where you can enjoy a drink while sitting in the water, tennis courts, and of course the casino. With its 400 rooms, there is nothing quaint about this place, but it does offer the utmost in comfort.

The **Royal Palm Beach Club** *(Private Club; ☎544-3737)* is set along the road linking Mullet Bay to Baie Nettlé, on the French side. Its modern high-rise buildings, whose parking lot was still under construction at the time of our visit, are right on the seaboard, giving some of the apartments an ocean view.

Nearby stands the **Cupecoy Beach Club** *(private club; ☎545-2243)*, which has a quiet, remote setting in a vast, little-inhabited landscape. It is located a mere stone's throw from Cupecoy Beach.

The **Towers at Mullet Bay** *(private club, ☎545-3069)* consists of several modern and somewhat sterile high-rises that lack charm. Though it is only a short distance from the beach, the only view it offers is that of fields stretching out to the horizon.

Cole Bay

Princess Port de Plaisance
US$290
≡, ≈, ℜ, K
Port de Plaisance, Union Rd.
☎544-5222
⇄544-2315
www.sxmhotels.com
By taking the road between Marigot and Philipsburg, you pass a sprawling resort, the Princess, whose buildings are spread throughout spacious, attractively landscaped grounds that are bordered by the Simson Bay Lagoon. The property, which is large enough to resemble a small city, includes 88 deluxe one- or two-room suites, which include, most notably, a kitchenette and a pleasant balcony overlooking the sea. There is also a private marina, all the services of a spa, a casino, a restaurant, tennis courts and shops. Despite its inordinate proportions, the Princess provides a pleasant stay, because it can cater to the every whim of its guests.

Little Bay

Next to Philipsburg lies Little Bay, a small cove with two hotels, slightly removed from the road, at the foot of sheer cliffs. The first of these establishments, the **Divi Little Bay Beach Resort** *(US$165; ≡, ≈, ℜ, ⊙; ☎542-2333, ⇄542-5150, www.diviresorts.com)*, lies at the bottom of a winding road that leads down to the bay. Its tidy layout makes the lovely setting very pleasant. It comprises a series of multi-storey cottages right by the sea, allowing guests to take full advantage of the beautiful ocean blue stretching out into the distance.

By retracing your steps and continuing west, you will come to the second of the two establishments, the **Belair Beach Hotel** *(US$375; ≡, K, ℝ; PO Box 140, Philipsburg,☎542-3362, ⇄542-5295, www.belairbeach.com)*. Built on a tiny patch of ground by the sea, it has a marvellous view of the water, while the road lies on the other side. The building, which has seen better days, is really nothing special, but provides adequate accommodation for vacationers who have come to take advantage of the beach, which is unfortunately very small. Every room has a dining area and a kitchenette.

Oyster Pond

Part of Oyster Pond Bay is French and part is Dutch. This is why some prices are listed in French francs and others in American dollars. **Don't forget: the area code for Saint-Martin is 590 and that of Sint Maarten is 599.**

There is an arm of land separating Oyster Pond from the sea, on which, until recently, there was just one hotel. In 2001, construction work completely altered the landscape and there is now a series of buildings housing condominiums. Change also touched Dawn Beach, as its hotel has closed its doors.

Sol Hotel
3,500 F per week
≡
Oyster Pond No. 38, 97150
☎***05.90.87.38.10***
⇄***05.90.87.32.23***
Located near the bay, Sol Hotel is a good place to stay in Oyster Pond. Housed in a white building that is well kept and perfectly charming with its lovely pastel balconies, the hotel offers guests suitably comfortable rooms.

Soleil de Minuit
US$170
≈, ≡, ℜ
☎***05.90.87.34.66***
⇄***05.90.87.33.70***
Soleil de Minuit was built on a hillside from which a panoramic view of the bay is captured at a glance. It goes without saying that this is a place of perfect tranquillity. The hotel offers charming rooms decorated with rattan furniture. The large patio, with a pool at the centre, is an ideal spot for relaxing and enjoying the view of the bay and its port.

Captain Oliver's
$US175, bkfst incl.
≡, ℜ
Oyster Pond, 97150
☎***05.90.87.40.26***
⇄***05.90.97.40.84***
Captain Oliver's is basically the heart of Oyster Pond, located on the shore of the bay on a lot adjoining the marina. Rooms are in small, well-kept pavilions, built rather close to one another and dispersed throughout the site. Its restaurant (see p137), which looks out onto the bay, is a pleasant spot for relaxing and admiring sailboats heading out for a day on the waves.

Mississippi
520 F
≈, ≡, ℜ
Oyster Pond, 97150
☎***05.90.87.33.81***
⇄***05.90.87.33.52***
The Mississippi is located in the hills surrounding Oyster Pond Bay. The rooms, embellished with a pretty wooden terrace, look out over the bay, allowing guests to soak up the picturesque countryside. With the sea at its feet, and isolated from the bay, the hotel is far from the hustle and bustle of the marina.

Colombus Hotel
980 F
≡, ≈, ℜ
☎05.90.87.42.52
⇄05.90.87.39.85
Not far from the marina, the Columbus Hotel consists of a few pink and turquoise buildings. While it is not luxurious, the establishment does offer comfortable, attractive rooms that are flanked by a pleasant balcony from which guests can admire the ocean.

Restaurants

Philipsburg

The largest concentration of fast-food restaurants on the island, including Kentucky Fried Chicken, Burger King and Pizza Hut, is found in Philipsburg, no doubt to serve the needs of travellers in a hurry. There are stalls downtown near the pier selling sausages, Mexican food and hamburgers, all of which must be eaten standing up. Those with more time, of course, can eat in one of the many restaurants in town. The tourist information booths can provide details about the local establishments, as well as give you with a few coupons offering reductions on drinks or meals.

Ric's Place
$-$$
69 Front St., just steps from Wathey Square
☎542-6050
The menu at Ric's Place is hardly inventive, but the Tex-Mex restaurant is convenient for those seeking a few moments' respite. It serves hearty meals like burgers and *chili con carne*, and has a lovely ocean view.

Kangaroo Court
$-$$
Hendrick Straat
☎542-4278
A veritable oasis of peace, Kangaroo Court has a magnificent interior courtyard adorned with a profusion of green plants, tables with parasols, and a fountain; indeed, the place offers patrons sanctuary from the never-ending bustle of Front Street. Another of the establishment's considerable assets: it is one of the few places where the menu does not feature burgers. Rather, it offers dishes prepared from healthy ingredients, such as quiches, salads and grilled-chicken sandwiches. In short, a pleasant eatery where you can enjoy a good lunch before resuming your shopping.

Reggae Café
$$
Wathey Square
Also facing the sea, this delightful café has an unpretentious, relaxed ambiance and tables on two terraces (one on each floor) looking out on the surf. The lovely warm hues of the decor are striking.

The Greenhouse
$$
☎*542-2941*
Continuing along Front Street, you'll come to Bobby's Marina, across from which stands the Greenhouse. Set back from bustling Front Street, this place offers much calmer surroundings. The menu is not very complicated: tuna salad, sandwiches and hamburgers. The charm of the Greenhouse lies mainly in its simple, friendly atmosphere, perfect for a meal with friends.

Pasanggrahan
$$-$$$
Front St.
☎*542-2743*
The little hotel Pasanggrahan (see p128) has a good seaside restaurant, part of which looks directly out on the beach. In a relaxed, unpretentious ambiance, it consistently serves quality dishes, like fried squid and grilled lamb chops.

L'Escargot
$$$-$$$$
Front St.
☎*542-2976*
One of the best restaurants in Philipsburg, L'Escargot has been prosperous and highly respected for no fewer than 25 years. The elegant dining room has no doubt contributed to its success, but it is above all the cuisine, especially the escargots, that charms its many diners.

Bec Fin
$$$-$$$$
141 Front St.
☎*542-2976*
One of Philipsburg's finest restaurants, the Bec Fin prepares excellent meals featuring lots of fish and shellfish. The traditional French cuisine will satisfy most tastes.

Antoine
$$$-$$$$
119 Front St.
☎*542-2964*
Another spot to keep in mind in Philipsburg is Antoine, where succulent French and Creole specialties are concocted. Among the best-known dishes of the house is the lobster,

always exquisitely presented. Excellent meat and poultry are among the other savoury selections. In addition to a delicious meal, guests enjoy a lovely view of the ocean from the dining room. The restaurant also serves good lunches.

Mullet Bay, Maho Beach and Cupecoy Beach

Cheri's Café
$$
☎545-3361
With its carefree atmosphere and location right in the heart of the tourist village, this place couldn't be friendlier and is always hopping. Crowds of people fill its outdoor terrace to enjoy a good meal and a good time. There is a bit of everything on the menu, from hamburgers to seafood.

The Globe
$$-$$$
Airport Rd.
☎544-2236
Located between Philipsburg and Maho Reef, The Globe is a charming roadside restaurant worth keeping in mind for its good, reasonably priced dishes of multinational inspiration. Among these are a few Japanese specialties, such as sushi, as well as Italian dishes. What's more, the decor is pleasant and the service courteous.

Boathouse Bar & Grill
$$-$$$
Airport Rd.
☎544-5409
Located right next to The Globe, and opening out onto the waters of the Simson Bay Lagoon, the Boathouse specializes in seafood, served in a pleasant atmosphere, despite the restaurant's proximity to the street.

Sushi
$$$
Hôtel Atlantis
Situated in the heart of the neon signs and loud, flashy decor of Maho Bay, the presence of Sushi appears almost surrealistic, so much does it clash with its immediate environment. Specializing in Japanese cuisine, as its name indicates, it is a pleasant place, peaceful and quiet. A good choice of sushi and *yakatori* dishes is offered at reasonable prices.

Paris
$$$
Set up in a quaint building facing the street, Paris is among the other noteworthy restaurants in the village. The menu, although not too sophisticated, does include a few good grilled fish and seafood dishes.

Oyster Pond

Captain Oliver's
$$-$$$
The restaurant at Captain Oliver's hotel not only offers a pleasant setting, particularly at the noon hour, but it also has a particularly tempting menu. The dining room looks out over the sea and the comings and goings at the marina. Although the view is probably the main reason to come here, the food, while not extravagant, is quite good. Salads and sandwiches are featured on the lunch menu.

Mississippi
$$$
The restaurant at the Mississippi hotel is pleasantly perched on a hillside. Guests enjoy a very beautiful setting while savouring simple but delicious dishes such as grilled steak or crab salad.

Entertainment

Philipsburg

Philipsburg is buzzing with activity during the day and though it attracts fewer visitors at night, there are still a few interesting bars.

In the midst of the Front Street bustle is an outstanding establishment, the seaside **Reggae Café** *(Wathey Square)*. It is just the place to have a drink in a friendly, laid-back ambiance.

The **Greenhouse** *(Bobby's Marina)* looks out onto the marina and welcomes patrons for a meal or just a drink. You can also come to shoot some pool on one of the tables. The atmosphere is laid-back and friendly.

Friday evenings, lovers of local music meet at the **Kangaroo Court** *(Hendrick Straat)*, which hosts some of the island's best musicians.

Mullet Bay

Cheri's Café is a huge outdoor bar set right in the middle of the tourist village. This is a great place from which check to out the action of the village while enjoying a drink. There is dancing as well.

If there is one must-see on the Dutch side of the island, it's definitely the **Sunset Beach Bar**. Located at the end of the landing strip at Princess Juliana Airport, it is the ideal place to watch the planes take off and land at the end of the day (particularly Thursdays, Fridays and Saturdays). Don't miss the landing of a 747...shivers guaranteed! This outdoor seaside bar is also a good place to contemplate the setting sun.

Another place for a good view of the sea and the setting sun is the **Baywatch** bar at the Caravanserai Beach Resort. Here, there is a large room, extremely well decorated room, bordered by windows overlooking the sea.

Casinos

Though there are casinos only on the Dutch side of the island, no fewer than a dozen occupy this small territory. Many of the hotels on the French side have free shuttle services for high-rolling guests looking for a little lady luck.

The biggest is the **Casino Royale**, located at the Maho Beach Hotel. You can try your luck at one of the 19 blackjack tables, six American roulette tables or two French ones, or get rid of your small change in one of the 250 slot machines.

The **Atlantis Casino** *(Cupecoy Bay)* welcomes guests into a sublimely decorated room. Once again there are baccarat, blackjack and poker (Caribbean stud poker), craps and roulette tables, as well as slot machines.

The other casinos, the **Dolphin Casino** *(Caravanserai Beach Resort)* and the **Golden Casino** *(Great Bay Beach Hotel)*, both have blackjack and poker (Caribbean stud poker) tables, slot machines and more.

The **Rouge et Noir** casino is the place for high rollers looking for unlimited stakes, as are the **Diamond Casino** and **Paradise Plaza**. All have baccarat, blackjack and poker (Caribbean stud poker) tables, as well as slot machines. Some offer a view of the sea.

Oyster Pond

To soak up the last rays of the sun in Oyster Pond, stop by **Captain Oliver's**. Its terrace, looking right out onto the bay, is the ideal spot from which to take in the dazzling sunset while sipping a drink and chatting.

Shopping

The Dutch part of the island is a true paradise for shoppers, since nothing is taxed.

Thus, shopping has become one of the most popular activities in Sint Maarten. Philipsburg is the best place to shop, and Front Street, its main street, is brimming with a jumble of upscale boutiques and affordable shops. Whether you're looking for jewellery, clothing or alcohol, take the time to compare the quality of the products at different shops before settling on anything.

Shops do not close at noon in Sint Maarten.

Philipsburg

Clothing

Sint Maarten T-shirts are among visitors' favourite souvenirs. There is an overwhelming selection of these in many of the shops on Front Street.

For elegant fashions, the **Ashburry** luxury boutique is recommended.

Designer shops, such as **Liz Claiborne**, **Polo Ralph Lauren** and **Tommy Hilfiger**, have shops on Front St. that present some of their namesakes' most beautiful creations.

Accessories

For bags, belts, hats and other accessories, stroll over to the **Summer Times** and **Little Switzerland** shops.

Jewellery and Porcelain

For luxurious jewellery and accessories that never fail to please lovers of beautiful objects who are not afraid to loosen their purse strings, **Ashburry, Colombian Emerald** (fabulous precious stones), **Little Switzerland** and **Oro de Sol** are the places to visit.

For less extravagant jewellery, try **New Amsterdam**.

Other stores on Front St. have a reputation for selling gold and silver jewellery at prices that approach bargain levels. It requires a bit of digging and negotiating, but the finds are often worth the effort. Among these shops, **Mirage** and **Shivas** are two locations to keep in mind.

Miscellaneous Souvenirs

Looking for a colourful souvenir, gift jewellery or an amusing knick-knack? Satisfaction awaits at the **American West Indies Company**

(Front St.) or at the charming **Greenwith** *(Front St.)* shop.

Fans of beautiful earthenware will find plenty of delightful items at the **Dutch Delft Blue Gallery** *(Front St.)*, which features very attractive pieces fashioned by Dutch artisans. Plates, curios, tiles and vases are just some of the objects you can purchase here.

Street vendors offer baubles and inexpensive souvenirs of all sorts.

Beauty Products

Many shops specialize in quality beauty products and, while there are not really any bargains to be found, the great selection on display merits a look. **Lipstick** and **Penha** on Front Street are good places to go.

Wines and Spirits

When it comes to affordable spirits, Sint Maarten is a small paradise for bargain-hunters. A few shops on Front Street are recommended, notably **Diamond**, **Rams** and **Caribbean Liquor and Tobacco**. There is also a **Caribbean Liquor and Tobacco** stand at Princess Juliana Airport.

St. Martin has only one typical liquor, Guanaberry, prepared from rum and a berry indigenous to the island. It is available, among other places, on Front Street at a shop simply called **Guanaberry**.

Mullet Bay

Clothing

Many little shops in Mullet Bay offer attractive selections of bathing suits and beachwear, notably **Canicule** and **Beach Bum**.

Children are catered to at **Margie Magic** *(Plaza del Lago)*, which sells tasteful clothing.

Miscellaneous Souvenirs

The Design Factory *(Plaza del Lago)* offers a lovely collection of decorative objects and hordes of other little souvenirs that are sure to please.

St. Barts

Touring the tiny islet of St. Barts, (formally known as Saint-Barthélemy) with its mere $25km^2$ of arid land, doesn't take much time.

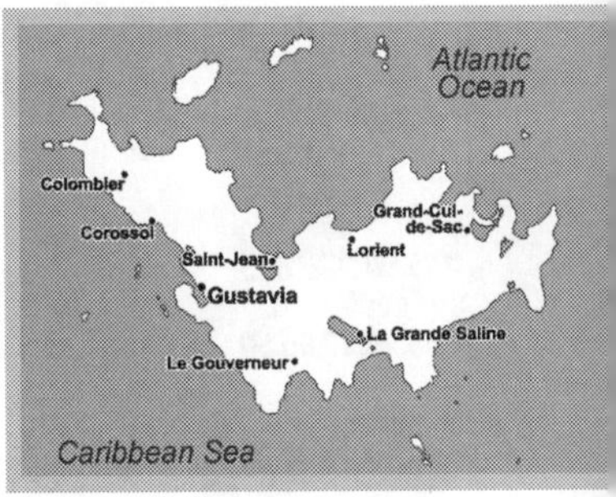

And yet, it encompasses so many captivating landscapes, enchanting villages composed of charming, Creole cottages and long, golden ribbons of sand bordered by azure waters, that visitors never tire of roaming its steep roads. St. Barts is as small as it is beautiful, and each parcel of land is maintained with infinite care so that nothing should mar its beauty. This flower of the Caribbean is every bit as compelling as its neighbours.

Finding Your Way Around

The island is criss-crossed by small, well-surfaced roads. A road passing by the airport links Gustavia to Saint-Jean. Another leads to Colombier, at the western extremity of the island. Yet another begins in Saint-Jean and goes through the eastern part of St. Barts, passing through Lorient, Anse du Grand Cul-de-Sac, Anse Toiny and Grande Anse. This same road runs back to Saint-Jean. A junction also allows travellers to reach Gustavia. In certain places, a few roads lead to isolated coves, notably those of Grande Saline and Gouverneur.

By Plane

The airport is located some 2km from Saint-Jean and Gustavia.

By Car

Car Rentals

Several car rental agencies have counters at the airport.

Avis
☎*05.90.27.71.43*
Budget
☎*05.90.27.66.30*

Europcar
☎*05.90.27.73.33*

Gumps Rental
☎*05.90.27.75.32*

Hertz
☎*05.90.27.71.14*

Island Car Rental
☎*05.90.27.70.01 or 05.90.27.62.55*

Smart of St. Barth
☎*05.90.29.71.31*

Scooter Rentals

If you would like to rent a car or a scooter, when leaving the parking lot (at the airport), turn left toward Saint-Jean or right toward Gustavia.

Chez Béranger
☎*05.90.27.89.00*

Dufau
☎*05.90.27.70.59*

By Taxi

There is a taxi stand at the airport: ☎05.90.27.75.81.

In Gustavia
☎*05.90.27.66.31*

Practical Information

Banque Française Commerciale
Rue du Général de Gaulle, Gustavia
☎*05.90.27.62.62*

Banque Nationale de Paris
Rue du Bord de Mer, Gustavia
☎*05.90.27.63.70*

Crédit Agricole
Rue Jeanne d'Arc, Gustavia
☎*05.90.27.89.90*

Galerie du Commerce
facing the airport, Saint-Jean
☎*05.90.27.65.88*

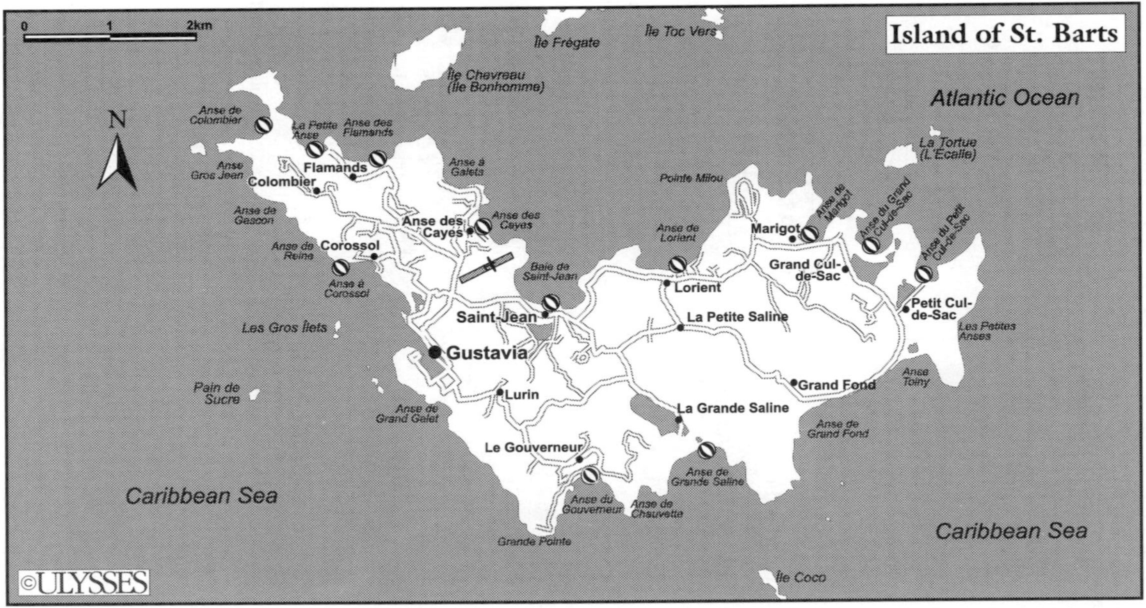
Island of St. Barts
0
1
2km
N
Île Frégate
Île Toc Vers
Île Chevreau
(Île Bonhomme)
Atlantic Ocean
La Tortue
(L'Écalle)
Anse de Colombier
La Petite Anse
Anse des Flamands
Flamands
Anse Gros Jean
Colombier
Anse à Galets
Pointe Milou
Anse de Gascon
Anse des Cayes
Anse des Cayes
Anse de Lorient
Marigot
Anse de Marigot
Anse du Grand Cul-de-Sac
Anse du Petit Cul-de-Sac
Anse de Reine
Corossol
Anse à Corossol
Baie de Saint-Jean
Lorient
Grand Cul-de-Sac
Petit Cul-de-Sac
Saint-Jean
La Petite Saline
Les Petites Anses
Les Gros Îlets
Gustavia
Anse Toiny
Grand Fond
Pain de Sucre
Lurin
Anse de Grand Galet
La Grande Saline
Anse de Grand Fond
Le Gouverneur
Anse de Grande Saline
Caribbean Sea
Anse du Gouverneur
Anse de Chauvette
Caribbean Sea
Grande Pointe
Île Coco
©ULYSSES

Post Offices

Gustavia

At the corner of Rue du Centenaire and Rue Jeanne d'Arc
☎***05.90.27.62.00***
Mon, Tue, Thu and Fri 8am to 3pm, Wed-Sat 8am to noon.

Saint-Jean

Galeries du Commerce
☎***05.90.27.64.02***
Manda, Thu and Fri 8am to 2pm, Wed-Sat 8am to 11am.

Lorient

☎***05.90.27.61.35***
Mon, Tue, Thu and Fri 7am to 11am, Wed and Sat 8am to 10am.

Medical Care

Hospital

☎***05.90.27.60.35***

Gendarmerie (inter-municipal police)

☎***05.90.27.60.12***

Police

☎***05.90.27.66.66***

Weather

☎***05.90.27.60.17***

Ocean Rescue

☎***05.90.27.70.41***

Attractions and Beaches

Travellers following the paved road that winds its way through the island will soon come across some of its most resplendent treasures: Gustavia, Anse de Grand Fond and Baie de Saint-Jean. To fully appreciate its charms, however, take the time to amble through its streets, to watch the frigates diving into its choppy waters, to feel the trade winds, to contemplate the sea shimmering beneath the sun, to watch time pass. The following tour will allow you to discover the deepest reaches of St. Barts.

Gustavia

The first colonists to settle on the island did so primarily to cultivate the land—a land whose sun-baked earth was the cause of much hardship. St. Barts had a

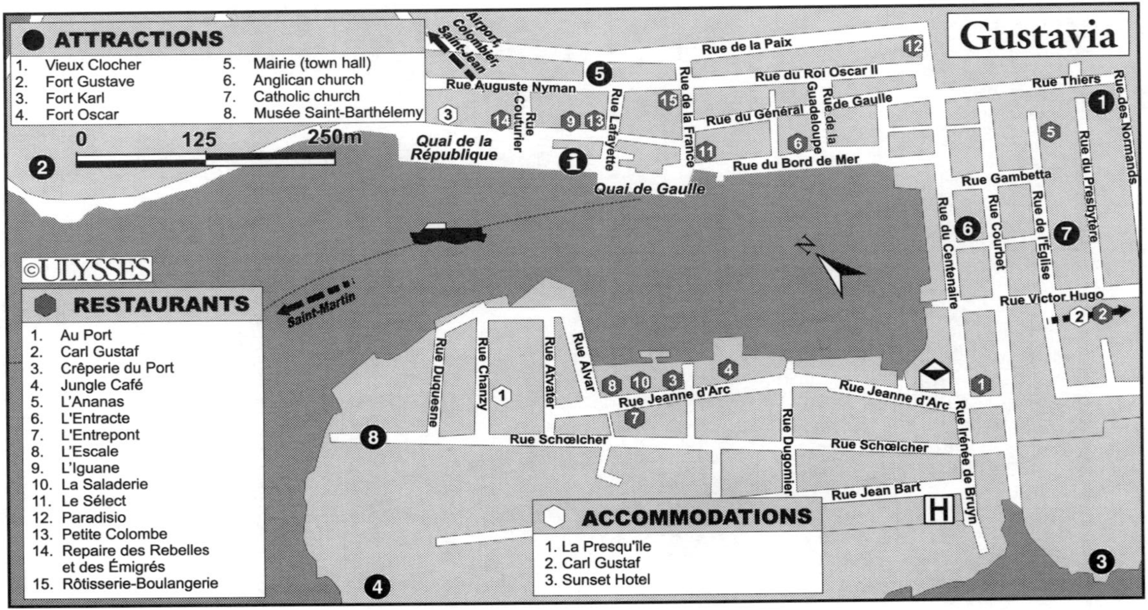
Gustavia
ATTRACTIONS
1. Vieux Clocher
2. Fort Gustave
3. Fort Karl
4. Fort Oscar
5. Mairie (town hall)
6. Anglican church
7. Catholic church
8. Musée Saint-Barthélemy
0
125
250m
©ULYSSES
RESTAURANTS
1. Au Port
2. Carl Gustaf
3. Crêperie du Port
4. Jungle Café
5. L'Ananas
6. L'Entracte
7. L'Entrepont
8. L'Escale
9. L'Iguane
10. La Saladerie
11. Le Sélect
12. Paradisio
13. Petite Colombe
14. Repaire des Rebelles et des Émigrés
15. Rôtisserie-Boulangerie
ACCOMMODATIONS
1. La Presqu'île
2. Carl Gustaf
3. Sunset Hotel
Airport, Colombier, Saint-Jean
Saint-Martin
Rue de la Paix
Rue du Roi Oscar II
Rue Auguste Nyman
Rue Couturier
Rue Lafayette
Rue de la France
Rue du Général de Gaulle
Rue de la Guadeloupe
Rue du Bord de Mer
Quai de la République
Quai de Gaulle
Rue Thiers
Rue des Normands
Rue du Presbytère
Rue Gambetta
Rue de l'Église
Rue Courbet
Rue du Centenaire
Rue Victor Hugo
Rue Duquesne
Rue Chanzy
Rue Atvater
Rue Alvar
Rue Jeanne d'Arc
Rue Schœlcher
Rue Dugomier
Rue Jean Bart
Rue Irénée de Bruyn

Vieux Clocher

ual development of a city. However, the pirates who were despoiling foreign ships attracted the wrath of the great powers, which was directed toward the residents of St. Barts. The expanding city was ultimately destroyed by the British in 1744.

Port Carenage, as it was then called, somehow managed to rise again from its ashes, and the city grew over the years. When St. Barts was ceded to Sweden in 1785 in exchange for France's right to trade with that country, the island retained its importance, but was renamed "**Gustavia**" ★★★ in honour of the Swedish king who reigned at the time. It prospered under the Swedes, and new buildings with a very different architecture were constructed. Unfortunately, few buildings from this period remain, having been destroyed by the fire that ravaged the island in 1852. The pretty green **Vieux Clocher**, or old bell tower, still stands on Rue du Presbytère. It once housed a bell cast in 1799, which rang off the important moments of the day. A clock has since replaced the bell.

particular asset, however, in that it had a natural harbour, well-sheltered from sea currents and winds, and thus ideal for mooring boats. This geographic feature was extremely advantageous for this tiny island, as colonists were able to establish an excellent port, where the many vessels plying the Caribbean could find safe haven. The pirates who were then sailing the seas were among the first to benefit from the port, and would dock in the calm waters of the Carenage harbour. Their presence, though perilous, was nevertheless beneficial to the islanders for a period, since this activity led to the grad-

At the end of the 18th and beginning of the 19th century, three forts were also built on the summits of the surrounding hills to protect the Swedish colony. The fortifications of only one of these stone forts, **Fort Gustave**, can be viewed today. Visitors will find a terrace offering a lovely **view ★** of Gustavia. Nothing remains of **Fort Karl**, while the fortifications of **Fort Oscar** have been modified over the years. This last site can only be observed from afar, as it is now occupied by the minister of armed forces.

When France retook possession of the island in 1878, Gustavia kept its name and its status as the principal town on the island, and the residents remained exempt from taxes. It is still the busiest and largest urban area in St. Barts. If you arrive by boat, you will find yourself more or less in the centre of town.

It is worth exploring the few streets radiating outward from the harbour, all lined with pretty little white houses topped by orange roofs. Wander about and explore Gustavia's charming back streets, enjoy its cafés and good restaurants, or give in to temptation and browse through its many shops. Besides the quaint houses, there are some distinguished edifices, like the ***Mairie*** (town hall) *(Rue Auguste Nyman)*, also called the Maison du Gouverneur, or governor's house, since the island's governors used to reside here. The stone foundation of this house supports a lovely green and white facade. Two other buildings are also worth a look. Built in 1885 of stone and wood, the **Anglican church** *(Rue du Centennaire)* is topped by a pretty bell tower. It still

St. Barts

Anglican church

serves a sizeable congregation. The church is located on one of the prettiest streets in town, **Rue du Centenaire** ★, which runs along the port, providing a good view of Gustavia. Meanwhile, the austere white facade of the **Catholic church** *(Rue de L'Eglise)*, the more imposing of the two, is visible in the distance from Rue du Centenaire.

You could spend a day visiting Gustavia's sights. If you are curious about the history, traditions and daily life of St. Barts, head to the **Musée Saint-Barthélemy** *(10 F; Mon 2:30am to 6pm, Tue-Fri 8:30am to 12:30pm and 2:30pm to 6pm, Sat 9am to 1pm; Wall House, corner of Alvar and Duquesne sts., ☎05.90.29.71.55)*, at the end of Gustavia point, which exhibits various objects evocative of an earlier time, when the Swedes and French settled here. This is a good opportunity to undertake a fascinating trip back through the history of the island's residents.

The streets bordering the natural harbour are very lively, as they are lined with pleasant shops, restaurants, the marina, and, of course, companies offering sea tours.

At the western end of the city is **Shell Beach**, a small beach which, as its name indicates, is covered in shells. Though it's not the nicest on the island, it is, nevertheless, extremely pleasant.

Follow Rue Auguste Nyman out of Gustavia, past the airport and into Saint-Jean.

Saint-Jean

The town of **Saint-Jean**★ lies stretched along the shore of the beautiful Baie de Saint-Jean. At first it seems like a town that does not amount to much more than several shopping centres, most notably the Galeries du Commerce, the Villa Créole and the Centre Commercial Saint-Jean. However, visitors will soon discover that this village has some lovely houses. Decorated with friezes and white balconies, they are built on the hillside and confer a great deal of charm to the village. Saint-Jean's main attraction is hidden behind lush vegetation: the **Baie de Saint-Jean** ★★, whose shimmering turquoise waters wash up onto a long crescent of golden sand. Virtual paradise for sun worshippers and swimmers, the bay is among the busiest beaches on the island. But don't let that stop you—this is hardly a noisy, bustling city, but rather a

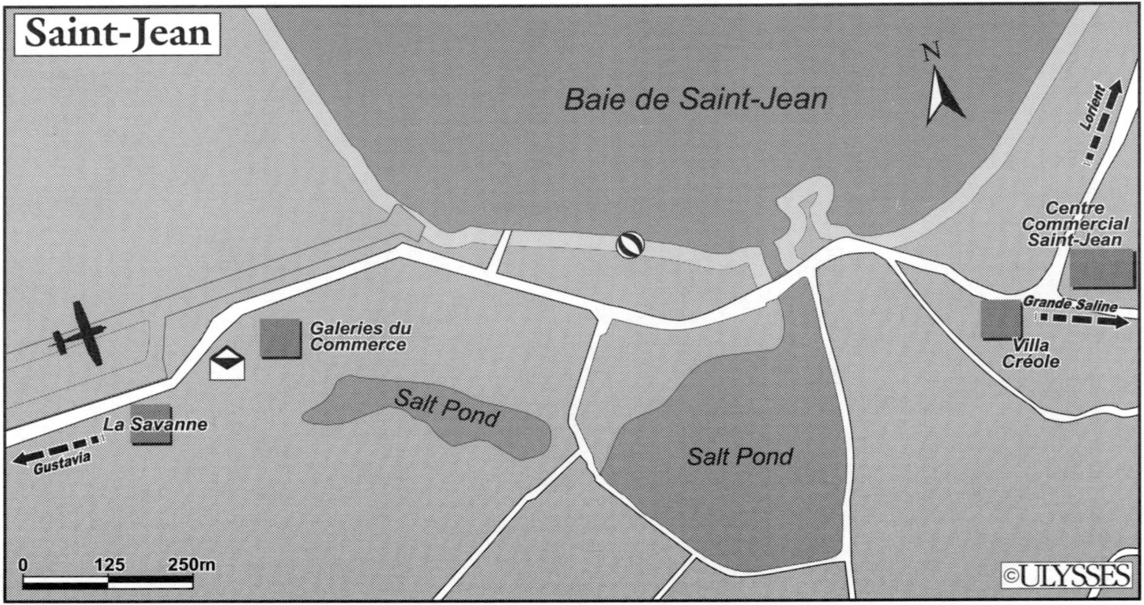
Saint-Jean
Baie de Saint-Jean
N
Lorient
Centre Commercial Saint-Jean
Grande Saline
Villa Créole
Galeries du Commerce
Salt Pond
Salt Pond
La Savanne
Gustavia
0
125
250m
©ULYSSES

pleasant place where an atmosphere of peace and tranquility reigns. Many people are also drawn by the considerable number of comfortable hotels standing at the water's edge (see p 160). In addition to the superb beach, there are many fine restaurants along the waterfront to be enjoyed in between swims (see p 170).

Continue toward Lorient.

Lorient

Though the route to **Lorient** follows the sea, all that is visible from the road is the vegetation surrounding the resorts and lovely homes. In certain places, the road opens up onto beautiful views of the precipitous coastline plunging into the sea. On your way into the village, you'll pass a grocery store, then a little cemetery whose tombstones are adorned with plastic flowers. This cute little hamlet lies on the shores of **Anse de Lorient** ★, which will definitely please surfing enthusiasts or those simply seeking a beautiful crescent of fine sand.

The road continues east to a less populated area of the island, making a loop as it passes the beautiful beaches of Anse du Grand Cul-de-Sac, Petit Cul-de-Sac and the magnificent southeastern coast.

Pointe Milou

This part of the island is dominated by sheer cliffs to which magnificent homes cling, benefitting from an unobstructed view of the choppy waters below. The place is quite secluded and perfectly quiet. A stroll through this fashionable district of St. Barts will certainly prove relaxing, but be forewarned: there are strong gusts of wind and visitors should refrain from touring the area on a moped.

Grand and Petit Cul-de-Sac

The eastern extremity of the island is on the windward coast. It is punctuated by intensely blue lagoons that lie at the bottom of sheer cliffs, well-sheltered from the wind and strong currents. Among these lagoons is the **Anse du Grand Cul-de-Sac** ★★, a beautiful cove where quaint orange-roofed houses are reflected in the crystal-clear waters, girdled by cliffs, making it a haven for windsurfing buffs and swimmers alike. Certain hoteliers have also wished to take advantage of this exceptional spot, and lovely resorts have been built here. Nevertheless, the area remains peaceful and not overly frequented.

Just a few steps from Grand Cul-de-Sac, nestled at the base of the hills, is **Anse de Marigot**. Steep cliffs rise up all around this lagoon, protecting it from the wind and making it a popular spot with both swimmers and small-boat owners, who moor their crafts in its calm waters.

Cabrette

East of Anse du Grand Cul-de-Sac, **Anse du Petit Cul-de-Sac** is even less developed. The undergrowth and seagrape trees growing here and there provide welcome shade from the hot sun and create the feeling of a deserted beach. Anse du Petit Cul-de-Sac has all the charm of a typical Caribbean beach far from the towns and free of any tourism development. No construction blots its landscape because the beach is covered in rocks of all sizes, making it impossible to swim there.

Anse Toiny

As the road continues, the landscape changes, with beaches of fine sand gradually giving way to steep cliffs. There are no fine-sand beaches in the southeastern part of the island; **Anse Toiny** and **Anse Grand Fond ★★** are bordered by sheer walls of rock continuously slammed by waves. The wild scene, which characterizes the *côte-au-vent* (windy coast), is rendered almost hypnotic by the huge, peaceful expanse of blue sea, only occasionally broken by a colourful boat going by. If you like rugged scenery, then take the time to visit this unspoiled region.

Alert travellers can catch sight of a typical St. Barts cottage, the **cabrette**, on the left side of the road, a little past the superb Le Toiny hotel (see p 165). A very low, small stone cottage, it was built to resist the wind's worst onslaughts.

The road follows the shore from Anse Toiny all the way to Anse Grand Fond before cutting inland. It snakes through the hills, climbs abruptly at times, then zigzags downhill between beautiful residences. Touring this part of the island by bike requires a lot of stamina. The region is sprinkled with charming little houses adorned with friezes and tiny gardens where rare cultivated island plants do their best to grow and flower. Dreamy and peaceful, this area typifies St. Barts perhaps more than any other.

In Petite Saline, the road splits in two, with one fork heading to Lorient and the other continuing inland; take the latter (keep left) and drive another kilometre, at most, to another fork; keep left to reach Anse de Grande Saline.

Anse de Grande Saline

Before reaching the ocean, you'll cross the interior and come upon the huge white rectangle formed by the cloudy water of the Grande Saline. In the past, salt was extracted from this saltern, endowing some residents of St. Barts with substantial returns. The Grande Saline is surrounded by a mangrove swamp and attracts many species of birds (especially waders), which can be observed by anyone with a pair of binoculars.

This saltern lends its name to the beach located nearby, **Anse de Grande Saline ★★**. Next to the swamp is a parking lot where visitors can leave their cars. A short path must then be taken, at the end of which a marvellous tableau awaits you: the azure ocean as far as the eye can see, and not a building in sight. This beach is renowned for its wild beauty, the lush green hills surrounding it, its fine sand and crystal clear waters. Far different from such touristy beaches as Baie de Saint-Jean, it is incomparably beautiful, its natural surroundings still untouched by any kind of development. Those who enjoy quiet swims and soft sand will be particularly contented.

To reach Gouverneur beach, retrace your steps toward Gustavia. In Lurin, a little village in the hills comprising a few cottages, you can take the road leading back down to the beach. Drivers should pay attention, however, for the road is poorly indicated; it is right next to the France Telecom buildings.

Anse du Gouverneur

The road goes down to the ocean, passing by small houses set in the middle of vast plots of land. Rather unpopulated, this rural region is strewn with somewhat wild vegetation. The road ends next to the vast property of a private residence, and visitors will have to leave their vehicles in the tiny parking lot or, as it is often full, by the side of the road. A very short path leads to the beautiful golden beach of the **Anse du Gouverneur ★★**, where gently lapping waves make swimming so inviting. No businesses blot the landscape of this wonderfully quiet cove, where only a single private dwelling borders the beach. With no merchants or parasol-renting kiosks (those with sensitive skin should provide for their own shelter), this beach is the quintessential small, forgotten Caribbean paradise.

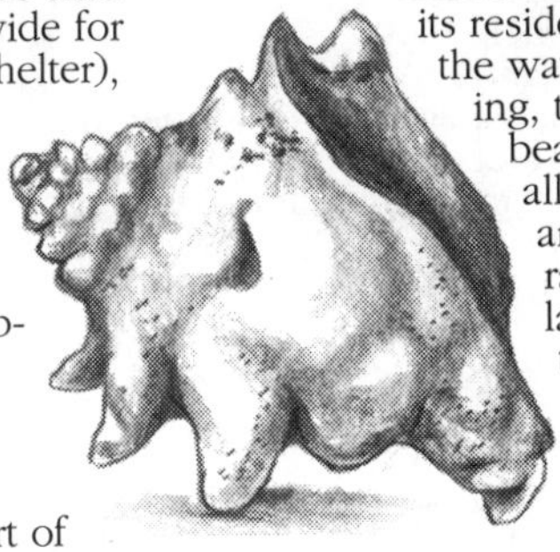

To visit the western part of the island, travellers must return to Gustavia. A few typical cottages line the road winding through the hills. From the top of these, looking down into the valley, you will see Gustavia: a multitude of orange roofs radiating out from the harbour, where all sorts of boats are moored.

To get to Corossol, retrace your steps and turn left onto the first road you come across. This road leads to Gustavia, from where it continues to Corossol.

Corossol

Corossol ★ is a tiny community that has developed on a hillside at the edge of **Anse de Corossol**. Here again, quaint little orange-roofed houses elegantly decorated with friezes brighten up an otherwise drab landscape of shrubs and undergrowth. Corossol has all the charms of yesteryear, a modest fishing village with the colourful fishing boats of its residents floating on the waves: it is a pleasing, typically Caribbean scene that is all the more pleasant because of its rarity on the island. Although the view is somewhat marred by the road running alongside the pretty beach, fortunately it gets little traffic. Corossol is truly lovely.

A small museum called the **Inter Ocean Museum ★** *(20 F; Tue-Sun 9:30am to 5pm; ☎05.90.27.62.97)* has opened here. It displays all kinds of shells (more than 400 varieties). This unique treasure was collected by the owner, Mr. Magras, over his lifetime.

To reach the centre of the island and the village of Colombier, return to the main road and turn left at the first intersection.

Colombier

This hamlet, high in the hills in the western part of the island, has been isolated for many years even though it is only 2km from Gustavia. Farmers in these parts had to work hard to reap meagre livelihoods from their unproductive lands. In 1918, Father De Bruyn wanted to help these deprived people, and thanks to his efforts a chapel, school and water tank were built. The chapel still stands at the centre of the village. Colombier enjoys a superb view from its perch up in the hills, where the land rolls away into the rippling waves of the sea.

At its very tip, you will find a path leading to **Grand Colombier ★★** beach, the last one at this extremity of the island. A 15min walk through some small shrubs will lead you to this beach, the most isolated on St. Barts. Once again, you will be enthralled by the quality of its sand, as fine as it is soft, bordering the crystal clear waters. This unparalleled tableau is yet another of the rapturous treasures of the magnificent islet that is St. Barts. Save some drinking water for the trek back to the parking lot, because you will have to climb uphill all the way back.

Head back down the northern coast of the island to Anse des Flamands.

Anse des Flamands

Anse des Flamands ★ is the most westerly beach on the island. It curves into a long crescent of white sand, and is dotted here and there by latania, trees whose large palm leaves are used to make hats and baskets. The peace and quiet of this beach make it an ideal spot for swimming and enjoying a siesta in the shade of a latania tree.

Anse des Cayes

Not far from Baie de Saint-Jean, **Anse des Cayes** has acquired quite a reputation for surfing. Those who dream only of sunbathing will also find its fine sand to their liking.

Outdoor Activities

With its 22 fine-sand beaches stretching along the Caribbean Sea and the Atlantic Ocean, St. Barts is a real paradise for water-sports enthusiasts. In fact, most of the island's outdoor activities are water sports. Besides enjoying the surf, however, you can go horseback riding and bicycling.

Swimming

If swimming is your thing, then all you have to do is pick the spot. Of the island's 22 beaches, 15 are great for swimming, and each is prettier than the last. The quality of the water at all of these beaches is monitored every year and found to be excellent (except at Gustavia, where it is average).

Beaches on the island are divided into two groups: those on the windward side, or *côte au vent*, and those on the leeward side, or *côte sous le vent*. Worth mentioning among the first are the beaches on Baie de Saint-Jean, Anse Lorient, Grand and Petit Cul-de-Sac, Anse Toiny and Anse de Grande Saline; these beaches are usually pounded by rough surf, although some are protected by natural breakwaters. The second group, includes the beaches of Anse Corossol, Anse Colombier, Anse des Flamands and Anse des Cayes; unlike the former, these beaches are usually calm. Finally, take note that there are no nudist beaches on St. Barts.

For sanitary reasons, dogs are not permitted on beaches.

Scuba Diving

The warm waters along the island's coasts provide an ideal environment for the development of coral, which in turn attracts all sorts of tropical fish. In order to protect these natural treasures, a marine nature reserve was created, most notably around the Fourchue and Frégate islands as well as the ocean floor off Anse du Grand Cul-de-Sac (encompassing Île de la Tortue) and Pointe Colombier. Depending on the zone, fishing is either limited or prohibited, making these sites fascinating for underwater sightseeing. This is why these areas have become prized among divers and a number of companies offer diving trips. Excursions are also offered to the island of Tintamarre (Saint-Martin) and Saba (Dutch Antilles; for experienced divers only). These expeditions include a boat trip and a picnic. It costs an average of about 300 F per dive, and 450 F to 500 F for a novice's first dive.

The following centres organize diving trips:

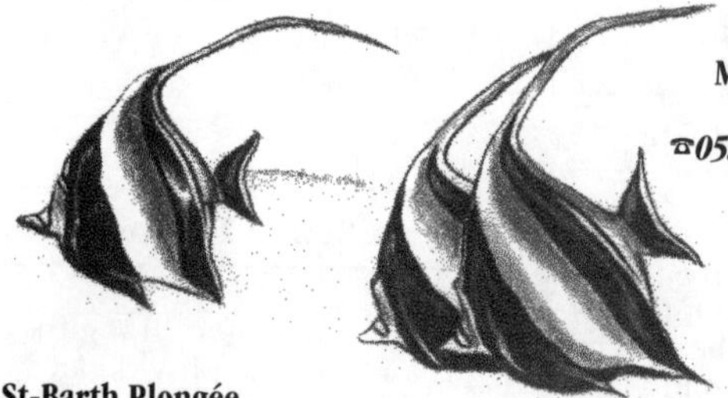

St-Barth Plongée
Port of Gustavia
☎*05.90.27.54.44*

West Indies Dive
Marine Service, Quai du Yacht, Gustavia
☎*05.90.27.70.34*

Mermaid Diving Centre
Hotel St. Barth Beach
☎*05.90.58.79.29*

Ocean Must
Rue Alvar, beside the museum
☎*05.90.27.62.25*

Scuba Diving Centre
Port de Gustavia
☎*05.90.54.66.14*

Snorkelling

The ocean depths boast magnificent natural scenery for those who dare venture underwater. If you are curious but do not wish to go scuba diving, renting snorkelling gear is an option:

Snorkelling Marina
Gustavia
☎*05.90.27.96.68*

Wind Wave Power
Anse du Grand Cul-de-Sac
☎*05.90.27.82.57*

Hookipa
Gustavia
☎*05.90.27.76.17*

Hookipa
Saint-Jean
☎*05.90.27.71.31*

Cruises

Excursions aboard sailboats and yachts are an enchanting way to explore the sea's sparkling waves. Some centres organize trips.

Marine Services
Gustavia Pier
☎05.90.27.70.34

Nautica FWI
☎05.90.27.56.50

Ocean Must
Quai de Gustavia
☎05.90.27.62.25

Windsurfing

The relatively quiet beaches of Grand Cul-de-Sac and Anse Saint-Jean, or the more exciting ones in Lorient, are particularly appreciated by windsurfers. Some enterprises along these beaches rent the necessary gear and offer lessons (rentals cost about 140 F per hour):

Wind Wave Power
Grand Cul-de-Sac
☎05.90.27.82 57

St-Barth Waterplay
☎05.90.61.38.40

St-Barth Yacht Club
☎05.90.27.70.41

Surfing

The Lorient beach is often battered by strong waves, making it an ideal place to surf. Intrepid surfers who have mastered their technique will enjoy Anse Toiny and its swelling seas.

Saint-Barth Waterplay
☎05.90.61.38.40

Reefer's Surf Club
☎05.90.27.67.63

Waterskiing

If you are in the mood to skim across the waves at high speeds, then waterskiing is for you. Mastering this activity does require some experience, but with a little patience and some good advice you should get the hang of it.

Master Ski Pilou
☎05.90.27.91.79

Personal Watercraft

If you get the urge to careen across the waves at full tilt, head to Anse du Grand Cul-de-Sac, where you can rent these water bound rockets. Because of the numerous accidents that have involved these machines, there is strict regulations governing their usage; note that it is prohibited to use them closer than 300m from shore. Count on paying 300F per half hour.

Mermaid Diving Centre
Anse du Grand Cul-de-Sac
Hôtel St. Barth Beach
☎05.90.58.79.29

Deep-Sea Fishing

Deep-sea fishing excursions not only offer the excitement of a big catch on the high seas, but also make for a fun outing. These trips usually last half a day. Equipment and fishing advice are provided.

Marine Service
Gustavia Pier
☎05.90.27.70.34

Ocean Must
Quai de Gustavia
☎05.90.27.62.25

Hiking

At the centre of tiny St. Barts, you'll find steep hills covered only with undergrowth and shrubs. Several roads run across these hills, but there are few hiking trails. Presently, there is only one in the region of Colombier. If you head off on a trek, make sure you are well equipped (good walking shoes, light-coloured clothing and food) and well-protected from the sun (sunscreen, sunglasses and a hat) to avoid sunstroke; leave early in the morning with plenty of food and water.

Bicycling

The island is criss-crossed by narrow roads that are often very steep and offer little shade. It is therefore not the ideal place for bicycling. However, a bicycle can be very useful for short distances. Rentals are available in several different spots.

Chez Béranger
Gustavia
☎05.90.27.89.00

Horseback Riding

A riding stable near Baie des Flamands organizes excursions on horseback. This is a pleasant way to discover another side of the island.

Ranch des Flamands
Baie des Flamands
☎05.90.62.99.30

Accommodations

Gustavia

The pretty town of Gustavia, with its shops, restaurants and marina, is always busy with visitors strolling about. With much to see and do, it is a pleasant place to pass the day, but there isn't much reason to spend the night, when the beaches and hills surrounding the city are so much more pleasant. There are only two hotels in the centre of town. One of these, the **Presqu'île** *(330 F; ≡, tv; Place de la Parade, 97133, ☎05.90.27.64.60, ⇄05.90.27.72.30)*, faces the marina and rents out a few basic rooms. This isn't a dream hotel, but it is well worth the affordable price.

Sunset Hotel
600 F
≡, tv
Rue de la République, B.P. 102, 97133
☎05.90.27.77.21
⇄05.90.27.81.59
The second hotel in the centre of Gustavia is the three-storey Sunset Hotel which also faces the marina. The rooms are well kept and more comfortable than the Presqu'île's, ensuring a good night's sleep.

Carl Gustaf
3,500 F bkfst incl.
≈, ≡, ℜ, K
Rue des Normands, 97133
☎05.90.27.82.83
⇄05.90.27.82.37
www.hotelcarlgustav.com
Part of a completely different category of establishment, the Carl Gustaf comprises a series of luxury villas built on a hillside away from the downtown area. Each villa has an exceptional view of the town's streets and the crystalline waves of the sea. To make the most of this superb location, each villa has a lovely terrace looking out over the beautiful landscape. These units are extremely comfortable and feature a small private pool and nicely decorated rooms

with big picture windows that frame the sea.

Saint-Jean

Saint-Jean is the second-largest town on St. Barts after Gustavia. The centre of the village proper actually consists of just a few small houses. All around, beautiful fine-sand beaches unfold, lined by hotels built to take full advantage of this superb location. The hotels are easy to find, since most are clustered together along the main road; each one, however, has its own vast property to provide guests with a measure of privacy.

Village St. Jean
1,000 F bkfst incl.
≈, ⊗
97133
☎05.90.27.61.39
⇄05.90.27.77.96
Village St. Jean is another comfortable establishment, nestled in the hills above Baie de Saint-Jean. It comprises several bungalows, attractively decorated with woodwork, spread out over a vast property. All have very lovely rooms, also adorned with attractive wood panelling. These rooms are airy and very simply furnished, but have an undeniable charm. In addition to enjoying the magnificent panorama, guests can take a luxurious dip in the large, tranquil swimming pool.

Tropical Hotel
1,080 F garden view
1,250 F sea view
≈, ≡, ⊗, *tv*
B.P. 147, 97095
☎05.90.27.64.87
⇄05.90.27.81.74
The Tropical Hotel is built on a hillside. To get there, take the road on your right on your way from Marigot (a sign indicates the way). The ideally located buildings offer an exceptional view of the blue sea stretched out below. The charming, well-maintained rooms are decorated with rattan furniture. Unfortunately, the hotel is not right on the beach, though a lovely pool makes up for this small drawback.

Hôtel Émeraude Plage
1,400 F
≡, ⊗, ℜ, *K*
97133
☎05.90.27.64.78
⇄05.90.27.83.08
www.emeraudeplage.com
The Hôtel Émeraude Plage stands in the midst of a huge garden facing Baie de Saint-Jean; it therefore boasts a delightfully peaceful setting and direct access to the beach. No fewer than 24 bungalows are spread out on either side of the garden, all with a view of the sea. Each is equipped

with a large area that opens out onto the garden and which functions both as a terrace and a well equipped kitchenette. This area is, in fact, an extra room that makes a good place to relax. The large bedrooms are equipped with wooden furniture and have a lovely decor, both simple and pleasant, which emits a sense of freshness. The property also has three suites and a villa.

Filao Beach Hotel
2,000 F garden view,
2,700 F sea view
≡, ⊗, *tv, K*
B.P. 667, 97099
☎05.90.27.64.84
⇄05.90.27.62.24
www.filaobeach.com
The pretty villas at the Filao Beach Hotel, a member of the prestigious Relais et Châteaux association, lie nearby. They are surrounded by a pleasant garden planted with trees and bushes of all kinds, ideal for strolling about and observing all the activity around the bird feeder. At the far end, you'll find a beautiful golden beach and the shimmering sea. You can drink in this beautiful sight while enjoying a meal on the hotel's terrace. This oasis of tranquility is the perfect place for a relaxing, restful holiday.

Tom Beach
2,200 F
≈, ≡
97133
☎05.90.27.53.13
⇄05.90.27.53.15
www.tombeach.com
Tom Beach has 12 bungalows spread over a small garden that opens onto a lovely beach. Each bungalow houses a large colonial-style bedroom, furnished with a magnificent canopied four-poster bed, beamed ceilings and shuttered windows. Each is decorated in lovely, vivid colours. In addition, each bungalow has a little yard with a hammock. The two largest bungalows look out over the sea.

Eden Rock
4,000 F
ℜ
97133
☎05.90.27.72.94
⇄05.90.27.88.37
www.edenrock.com
You can't miss Eden Rock, a luxurious property with buildings that reign over Baie Saint-Jean. It is reached, with some difficulty, via a steep dirt road that climbs up the rock, where some of the rooms are located in buildings surrounded by a profusion of plants. The view from here is exquisite. The other rooms are located in beachfront buildings, also on the rock. Particular attention was given to the decoration

of the rooms, with antique furniture and lace curtains. Each has individual flair and an ocean view.

Lorient

By following the main road, you'll come upon Lorient, a small hamlet with just a few houses. The beach of Anse Lorient and the charming hotels lie nearby.

La Normandie
450 F
≈, ≡
97133
☎***05.90.27.61.66***
⇄***05.90.27.98.83***
La Normandie is located by the road, in a less-than-enchanting setting. It does, however, offer reasonably priced rooms, which are well-maintained and quite comfortable, though hardly charming. The establishment also boasts a little garden with a small swimming pool.

Manoir de Saint-Barthélemy
650 F
≈, K
97133
☎***05.90.27.79.27***
⇄***05.90.27.65.75***
If there is one truly unique hotel property in St. Barts, Manoir de Saint-Barthélemy is certainly it. In a vast, magnificent garden lies a 17th-century Breton manor that was transported to the island and rebuilt beam by beam; this building houses the hotel's main hall. The rooms are fitted out in wooden bungalows whose architecture echoes that of the manor. They are very large and magnificently decorated with tasteful antique furniture. The bed, for instance, is draped in a white mosquito net, giving it the romantic appearance of yesteryear. A feeling of well-being emanates from these rooms, and the meticulous attention to detail at this establishment—one without equal in St. Barts—is a real treat. And for the price, it is truly a bargain.

Les Mouettes
990 F
⊗, K
97133
☎***05.90.27.77.91***
⇄***05.90.27.68.19***
Travellers can rent one of the small white cottages at Les Mouettes, whose property reaches right down to the ocean's blue waters. Each villa is equipped with a balcony overlooking the sea, a simple yet lovely decor and a kitchenette. Moreover, the beach's proximity makes the place a great vacation spot.

Hôtel La Banane
2,000 F bkfst incl.
≈, ℜ, ≡
97133
☎***05.90.27.68.25***
⇄***05.90.27.68.44***
www.labanane.com
This hotel's rooms are all set up inside pretty, colonial-style Creole houses, giving it a special character. The shutters, wooden walls and rustic, old-fashioned furniture fit right in, lending the place a comfortable, homey feel.

Around Lorient

Hostellerie des 3 Forces
$US200
≈, ≡, ⊗, ℜ
Vitet, 97133
☎***05.90.27.61.25***
⇄***05.90.27.81.38***
Hostellerie des 3 Forces is a friendly establishment built right in the mountains, in very quiet surroundings, far from the city and the tourism scene. The rooms are in lovely wooden cottages, fitted out with balconies where guests can contemplate their surroundings. They are simply furnished, but comfortable. To reach the hotel, follow the signs from Lorient.

Pointe Milou

Past Lorient, the road winds along the hillside with signs leading to Pointe Milou. This road is very steep and seems to lead nowhere, but don't despair; upon reaching the bottom of the cliff you will come upon the beautiful buildings of the **Christopher Hotel** *(2,600 F; ≈, ≡, ℜ; B.P. 571, 97098, ☎27.63.63, ⇄27.92.92)*. The site consists of a series of oceanfront buildings terraced into the cliff side. The rooms are impeccably maintained and adorned with elegant furniture. Each of them has a large terrace overlooking the sea and a lovely bathroom. Though the beach is somewhat rocky, the site itself is pleasantly laid out, with a huge private terrace and a magnificent swimming pool at guests' disposal.

Anse du Grand Cul-de-Sac

The beach at Anse du Grand Cul-de-Sac is the prettiest in this part of the island, and several hotels have been built here to take advantage of this beautiful, isolated crescent of golden sand. Far from all the hustle and bustle, this beach is a real vacation paradise.

Résidence du Bois l'Angélique
750 F
≈, ≡, ⊗, *K*
97133
☎***05.90.27.92.82***
⇄***05.90.27.96.69***

The Résidence du Bois l'Angélique has been designed so that guests can benefit from a splendid view of the silvery waters of Anse du Grand Cul-de-Sac stretching out into the distance. Every room has a charming terrace opening out on this magnificent tableau. Each has a simple and airy decor, quite pleasant for those seeking shelter from the hot rays of the sun.

El Sereno
1,400 F bkfst incl. garden view
1,500 F bkfst incl. sea view
≡, ≈, tv, ℜ
B.P. 19, Grand Cul-de-Sac 97095
☎05.90.27.64.80
⇄05.90.27.75.47
www.serenobeach.com

El Sereno's rooms are housed in pavilions built in the heart of a charming garden. Each is pleasantly decorated and has a terrace with rattan furniture looking out over the shady, verdant surroundings. The pool and restaurant are located on a terrace lookout overhanging the waves of Grand Cul-de-Sac. This wonderfully tranquil spot affords magnificent views of the seascape.

Résidences Saint-Barth
1,485 F
≡, ≈, ℜ, ⊙, K
B.P. 81, 97098
☎05.90.27.85.93
⇄05.90.27.77.59

Near the St. Barths Beach Hotel, and part of the same hotel complex are the Résidences Saint-Barth. Built on the hill overlooking the bay, the 21 one-, two- and three-room villas all have big bay windows and a pretty terrace from which to enjoy the stunning landscape. No fewer than seven little pools are at guests' disposal.

St. Barths Beach Hotel
1,500 F
≈, ≡, ℜ, ℝ
B.P. 580
97098
☎05.90.27.60.70
⇄05.90.27.77.59
www.stbarthbeachhotel.com

Though the garden at the St. Barths Beach Hotel can hardly be described as superb, as it is practically non-existent, the beachfront buildings have a pleasant setting. Moreover, all the rooms have a little balcony overlooking the sea. The large, well-kept and simply decorated rooms offer decent comfort without being luxurious. The proximity of the sea lends the place a pleasant beach-vacation ambiance.

Guanahani
2,280 F bkfst incl.
≡, ≈, ⊗, tv, K
B.P. 609, 97098
☎05.90.27.66.60
⇄05.90.27.70.70

Upon entering the Guanahani property, you

will first be charmed by the profusion of flowering plants. Then, here and there on the grounds, you will discover lovely Creole-style cottages decorated with vibrant colours. Each has a terrace, and the fancier ones have a private pool or a whirlpool bath. The sea unfurls at the far end of the garden. The main building, where the lobby is located, looks out over an endless seascape.

Anse Toiny

Le Toiny
3,960 F
≡, ≈, ⊗, *tv*, *K*, ℜ
97133
☎05.90.27.88.88
⇄05.90.27.89.30
Anse Toiny is located on the steepest shore of the island, and the rough surf makes swimming impossible. It was here, in front of the unbridled sea, that the owner of Le Toiny chose to build a luxurious hotel offering unparalleled comfort. Luxurious villas with magnificent wood floors, elegant furniture, and wonderfully bright, airy rooms make guests feel at home. Everything is impeccable, even the bathrooms. The best thing about these villas is that the rooms all open onto a terrace with a private pool. A cut above the rest, Le Toiny boasts an exceptionally peaceful setting.

Colombier

P'tit Morne
1,000 F
≈, ⊗, *K*
97096
☎05.90.27.62.64
⇄05.90.27.84.63
Past Colombier, at the very end of the road, is P'tit Morne. Perched atop a hill, this establishment benefits from an unobstructed view of the ocean, stretching out to the horizon. To make the most of this splendid landscape, every room has a large balcony—almost an extra room in itself!—where you can relax and contemplate the sea from afar. The rooms, simply furnished and sombrely decorated, are very well maintained and perfect for those seeking decent accommodations that don't cost a fortune. Good value.

François Plantation
2,700 F
≡, ≈, *tv*, ℜ
97133
☎05.90.29.80.22
⇄05.90.27.61.26
www.francois-plantation.com
The adorable village of Colombier is located in the hills in the western part of the island. Erected on the outskirts of this peaceful village, the hotel François Plantation stands on a vast property planted with trees and flowering shrubs that

offer welcome shade. At the heart of this verdant vegetation, you'll find a number of cozy, colourful bungalows. All have comfortable, beautifully decorated rooms furnished in the colonial-style. Some look out onto the garden, while the more expensive units afford an endless view of the sea. You'll discover an oasis of serenity here.

Anse des Cayes

Nid d'Aigle
450 F
≈
97133
☎05.90.27.75.20
⇄05.90.27.51.10
Nid d'Aigle is a pleasant, friendly and inexpensive place on the hill overhanging Anse des Cayes. It offers simple rooms bereft of any superfluous luxury. Only the bare essentials are provided: a bed, a small bathroom and a cupboard. The establishment is clean, however, and has an exceptional location with a stunning view. Moreover, the large terrain allows guests to fully enjoy this landscape.

Yuana
1,200 F
≈, ≡, ⊗, K
97133
☎05.90.27.80.84
⇄05.90.27.78.45
www.yuana.com
Yuana is a lovely establishment facing the ocean stretching out into the distance. Perched atop a hill, it consists of several bungalows housing comfortable rooms, charmingly appointed with rattan furniture in pleasing pastel shades.

Manapany
2,300 F bkfst incl.
≡, ≈, ⊛, ⊗, tv, ℜ
B.P. 114, 97133
☎05.90.27.66.55
⇄05.90.27.75.28
www.lemanapany.com
The Manapany hotel's villas lie right at the heart of the tiny, charming cove of Anse des Cayes. The white buildings have large bay windows overlooking the sea and comfortable rooms. The hotel's garden is a lovely place to stroll in peace, far from the hustle and bustle.

Anse des Flamands

Anse des Flamands is the last long beach on the northwestern side of the island. A few hotels have taken advantage of this beautiful and secluded natural site.

Auberge de la Petite Anse
700F
≡, *K*
B.P. 153, 97133
☎05.90.27.64.89
⇄05.90.27.83.09
At the very end of Flamands Bay stand the bungalows belonging to the Auberge de la Petite Anse, which seem to cling to the cliff's edge. The 16 charming bungalows are not flashy, but offer all the comforts (each has a kitchenette) and are set on pleasant grounds.

Baie des Anges
1,300 F
≈, ≡, ℜ, *K*
B.P. 162, 97133
☎05.90.27.63.61
⇄05.90.27.83.44
Baie des Anges is set in a very lovely sky-blue, wooden-slat building. The living quarters, all of which come with private terrace, have splendid ocean views and large rooms decorated with colourful rattan furnishings. Moreover, the establishment has a lovely swimming pool out on the cliffside. The idyllic site is far from the bustle, surrounded by nothing but the ocean which stretches as far as the eye can see.

St-Barth Isle de France
4,400 F bkfst incl.
B.P. 612, 97098
☎05.90.27.61.81
⇄05.90.27.86.83
The beautiful buildings of the St-Barth Isle de France lie nearby. The main house was built right at the edge of the shimmering sea; to take full advantage of this stunning setting, it has a large terrace overlooking the idyllic landscape. The guest rooms are not located in this building, but in villas scattered throughout the large property. Even though they were not built right by the sea, special touches, like their beautiful old-style furnishings, of the kind that used to be found on the islands, lovely draperies and large bay windows create a very pleasant ambiance nonetheless.

Restaurants

Gustavia

You won't have any trouble finding a good restaurant in Gustavia, especially at lunch time, when the terraces open up and good daily specials top the menus.

Rôtisserie-Boulangerie
$
☎05.90.27.66.36
On Rue du Roi Oscar II, you'll find the Rôtisserie-Boulangerie, where you can stock up on bread and deli foods for a picnic. They have sandwiches of all

kinds, roast chicken, delicious pastries and juices; if you feel like spoiling yourself, there are also Fauchon products, imported from France, to choose from.

Petite Colombe
$
Rue Lafayette
☎05.90.27.93.13
La Petite Colombe offers a good selection of Viennese bread and buns, pastries and sandwiches, making it an ideal place for breakfast or lunch.

L'Entracte
$
Rue du Bord de Mer
☎05.90.27.70.11
This unpretentious little restaurant overlooks the marina. The entrance is indicated by a huge poster of Che Guevara. This is the place to go for a quick bite; the menu includes hamburgers and pizza.

Le Sélect
$-$$
Rue de la France
Le Sélect is the perfect spot if you're craving a burger and fries. These can be enjoyed in the outdoor dining area, set in a garden giving onto the street. The place is not among the most enchanting in Gustavia, but it does have a friendly atmosphere.

Visitors will find many establishments near the port in which to grab a bite to eat or enjoy a good meal in a relaxed atmosphere. Among these is the **Crêperie du Port** *(**$$**; Rue Jeanne d'Arc)*, which offers a good selection of stuffed crepes.

La Saladerie
$$
Rue Jeanne d'Arc
If you would rather partake of a simple, fresh meal, head to La Saladerie instead. The menu offers no extravagant dishes, but the salads (with paper-thin slices of smoked ham or warm goat cheese) and pizzas are always good. You can savour these while enjoying the activity around the port of Gustavia all day long.

L'Escale
$$-$$$
Rue Jeanne d'Arc
☎05.90.27.81.06
Right next door, L'Escale is a very popular restaurant both at lunch and dinner. This place is a favourite because of its laid-back and friendly ambiance and its wonderful view of the port. The menu is hardly ground-breaking, featuring such fare as pizza cooked in a wood-burning oven and pasta au gratin. The food is good—if a little pricy.

L'Entrepont
$$-$$$
Rue Jeanne d'Arc
☎ ***05.90.27.90.60***
The decor at L'Entrepont evokes the sea: azure and white walls decorated with buoys and other marine objects. Its only roof are the leaves on the tall trees and the awning that is rolled out when necessary. Its casual ambiance is extremely inviting. The menu, good, generous and reasonably priced, includes a complete meal (appetizer, main dish and dessert) for 100 F or 150 F. This is clearly a good option to know about in the city.

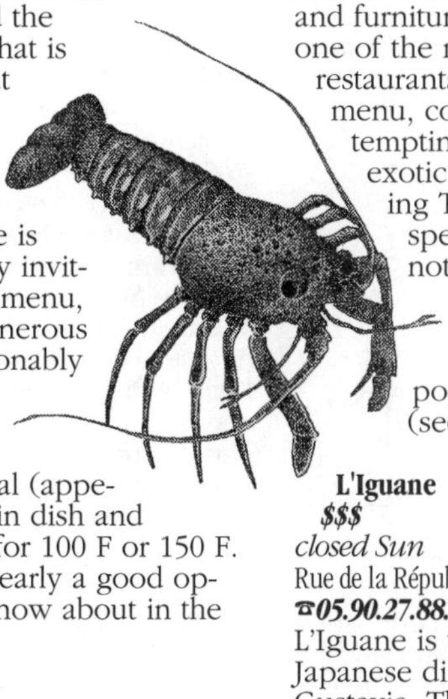

L'Ananas
$$$
from noon
Rue de l'Église
Located far from all the action at the port, l'Ananas is a charming French restaurant whose terrace is practically hidden by vegetation. People come here for a quiet lunch, where they can enjoy unpretentious dishes such as salads and pizzas. In the evening, a full range of dishes is offered, and patrons will have much to choose from among a variety of fish and seafood dishes.

Jungle Café
$$$
noon to midnight
Rue Jeanne d'Arc
Jungle Café, adorned with a host of colonial-style objects and furniture, is definitely one of the most charming restaurants in the city. The menu, composed of a tempting variety of exotic dishes, including Thai and Chinese specialties, is also notable. Open for both lunch and dinner. The place is also a popular bar (see p 175).

L'Iguane
$$$
closed Sun
Rue de la République
☎ ***05.90.27.88.46***
L'Iguane is the place for Japanese dining in Gustavia. The menu here consists primarily of sushi and sashimi, which are welcome and delicious culinary experiences on a hot day.

Repaire des Rebelles et des Émigrés
$$$
Rue de la République
☎ ***05.90.27.72.48***
The main reason to go to the Repaire des Rebelles et des Émigrés is its beautiful dining room, opening on

the marina and fitted out with wooden furniture and lush green plants; it exudes a subdued ambiance of luxurious holidays at the beach. The ambiance is perfect for lunch, when clients can enjoy watching the bustle in the streets. The place is just as pleasant in the evening, when the menu displays consistently delicious fish and seafood dishes in addition to its lunch-time fare. Breakfast is also served here.

Paradiso
$$$-$$$$
lunch and dinner
closed Sat and Sun
Rue Oscar II
The menu at the Paradiso reads thus: "*This menu changes with the deliveries, the catch of the day and the boss's mood*"—a guarantee that the food is always perfectly fresh. A few dishes appear regularly on the menu, such as the succulent and delightfully unique sea bream medallions in Creole sauce or rock lobster medallions with lentils. The boss, for his part, ensures that service is always attentive.

Au Port
$$$-$$$$
Mon-Sat from 7pm
Rue du Centenaire
☎05.90.27.62.36
For many years a highly reputed restaurant in Gustavia, Au Port will delight diners as much with its charming dining room as with its dishes, which are always succulent. The menu is bound to make it difficult to choose between its French specialties (red snapper with ginger) and Creole dishes (goat *massalé*), which are equally delectable.

Carl Gustaf
$$$$
lunch and dinner
Rue des Normands
☎05.90.27.82.83
Outside of downtown Gustavia, you can try the restaurant at the Carl Gustaf hotel, which serves elaborate dishes prepared with finesse. The chef combines French culinary techniques and regional ingredients, particularly those from the sea. While dining, guests can enjoy an unparalleled view from the magnificent terrace overlooking the sea and marina.

Saint-Jean

Rôtisserie-Boulangerie
$
Villa Créole
☎05.90.27.73.46
In the Villa Créole, at the centre of Saint-Jean, you'll find the Rôtisserie-Boulangerie, a specialized grocer. Like its counterpart in Gustavia, it sells sandwiches and roast chicken.

La Créole
$$
Villa Créole
La Créole, in the heart of the Villa Créole, is a good spot for lunch, when a good, reasonably priced daily special (veal kidney with mustard sauce for 60F or tuna steak for 65F) is offered. If this does not appeal to you, note that à la carte dishes, including delicious salads, are available.

La Plage
$$-$$$
Hôtel Tom Beach
☎05.90.27.53.13
Set right by the sea, to the point where some tables are actually in the sand, La Plage is a very pleasant restaurant, particularly at lunchtime. It is even better because it allows you to enjoy a good meal without losing sight of the sea while the sun is at its peak. On the menu is a nice variety of dishes, including salads and Creole or cheese dishes, deliciously prepared, if somewhat pricey.

Le Pélican
$$$
lunch and dinner
Saint-Jean
☎05.90.27.64.64
Not far from the Villa Créole, Le Pélican is advantageously situated on the waterfront. This no doubt explains why companies offering island tours bring their customers here for lunch. The place gets quite busy, and this popularity does have its disadvantages: come at lunch time and you'll invariably get stuck inside, since the terrace overlooking Baie de Saint-Jean is always packed. The acclaim of this eatery is also due to its menu, which includes tasty dishes like mussels, chicken with mustard sauce and crab salad.

Hostellerie des 3 Forces
$$$
☎05.90.27.61.25
Past Lorient, watch for a sign on your right that marks the road to follow. Deep in the country, far from the action of the city, the restaurant at the Hostellerie des 3 Forces enjoys a wonderfully tranquil setting. The place is perfectly secluded at nightfall, except for the few souls who have ventured off the beaten path. Here, you can savour dishes that the owner claims have not changed over the last 15 years. Every one of them is, of course, among the classics of French cuisine, notably the *magret de canard* (breast of duck) and the brochette of fish that are always good, if not particularly innovative.

Eden Rock
$$$-$$$$
lunch and dinner
☎05.90.27.72.94
At the restaurant at Eden Rock, you can savour fish or seafood dishes in a styl-

ish and friendly atmosphere that is quieter than that of Le Pélican's, situated nearby. The restaurant is located in a splendid, elegantly decorated wooden building overlooking the ocean. The food is somewhat pricey, but the location is well worth the expense.

Filao
$$$$
breakfast and lunch
☎05.90.27.64.84
If you're looking for quality French cuisine, you must try the restaurant at the Filao hotel. You'll be treated to fine food, all the while enjoying the beautiful panoramic view.

Lorient

K'fé Massaï
$$$-$$$$
☎05.90.29.76.78
Located by the road, beyond the large centres of tourism, it would be easy to miss the K'fé Massaï. The restaurant is hidden away in an earth-coloured building beside a parking lot and rows of bushes. Upon entering, you suddenly feel far away from the Caribbean, somewhere in Africa. The decor, made up of masks, sculptures and plants, succeeds in evoking this distant land. The huge dining room has sofas, some comfy arm chairs and tables where you can enjoy a leisurely meal. The noteworthy menu is inspired by French culinary traditions, but each meal is originally prepared. Very different from the other restaurants on the island, K'fé Massaï is worth the trip to Lorient.

Anse du Grand Cul-de-Sac

Le Rivage
$$-$$$
lunch and dinner
☎05.90.27.82.42
Le Rivage sits at the water's edge, with its windows open to the sea so that diners can enjoy the vast expanse of shimmering blue while they savour good French and Creole meals. Among the Creole dishes are traditional *accras*, grilled fish and *boudin créole.* This restaurant is tailor made for those who want to try some Creole specialties in an enchanting environment.

Gloriette
$$$
☎05.90.27.75.66
Also located on the beach, Gloriette is one of the island's fine-dining Creole restaurants. Come here for the culinary experience, but also for the splendid location, which is equally captivating. The dining room,

though decorated with restraint, is very attractive. The overall design highlights the magnificent tableau of the ocean, extending as far as the eye can see.

Boubou's
$$$
Hôtel El Sereno
☎*05.90.29.83.01*
Overlooking the sea, Boubou's is beautifully set. The furniture, somewhat exotic with its spotted or striped fabric, adds to the charm of the place. In fact, the setting is the real reason to come here as the menu, though adequate, is hardly extraordinary.

Sushi's
$$$-$$$$
☎*05.90.29.83.26*
Sushi, that Japanese specialty of rice and raw fish that is both fresh and healthy, is just the right dish to enjoy in the tropics. And Sushi's prepares good sushi. It also serves other Japanese specialties, including *yakitori* and *sashimis*. Dine in the attractive dining room, with a view of the ocean.

Anse Toiny

Le Gaïac
$$$$
lunch and dinner
Hôtel Le Toiny
☎*05.90.27.88.88*
When you arrive at Le Gaïac, a gourmet restaurant, you will be welcomed into a tastefully decorated dining room, adorned with large windows looking out onto Anse Toiny. A quick survey of the menu is enough to make you hungry. How to choose between such a vast selection of dishes, each more tempting than the last, like the large rock lobster coated with gingerbread or the *poêlée de Saint-Jacques aux échalotes et aux aubergines vinaigrées* (panfried scallops with shallots and eggplant). The meal will live up to your expectations and you'll leave with fond memories of your evening at Le Gaïac.

Anse de Grande Saline

Les Salines
$$-$$$
Grande Saline's beach is definitely one of the loveliest on the island, even more so because it is some distance from the island's tourism hot-spots and still pretty undeveloped. This isolation has its inconveniences: at lunch, it's hard to find something to eat. Luckily, just steps from the beach is Les Salines, which offers simple but good dishes, like salads, a merguez (small, spicy sausage) and fries plate or a daily special, of course.

Pleasant, relaxed atmosphere.

Colombier

Petite Colombe
$
☎05.90.27.95.27
A lovely bakery/cake shop, Petite Colombe makes good sandwiches which can be enjoyed at one of the plastic tables on the eatery's miniscule terrace. Breakfast is also served here.

François Plantation
$$$$
dinner only
☎05.90.27.78.82
The restaurant in this hotel has a large dining room decorated with beautiful wooden furniture, rattan chairs and large picture windows that open onto the garden, creating a warm ambiance. In this refined setting, patrons are treated to carefully prepared meals, worthy of the best French kitchens.

Anse des Caves

Fellini's
$$$-$$$$
Hôtel Manapany
☎05.90.27.66.55
The elegant Manapany hotel houses a wonderful restaurant whose delicious dishes are inspired by the gastronomic traditions of Italy. Artistically prepared, these specialties are something to savour. The elegantly decorated dining room overlooks the ocean.

Anse des Flamands

La Langouste
$$-$$$
Baie des Anges hotel
Flamands Beach
☎05.90.27.63.61
There's nothing like a fresh lobster salad for lunch, enjoyed by the pool overlooking the ocean. This is the scene that awaits you at La Langouste. Perfect for lunch, it is no less enchanting at night, when the menu is somewhat more refined, featuring always delicious and reasonably priced French and Creole specialties.

Case de l'Isle
$$$-$$$$
lunch and dinner
☎05.90.27.81.61
Case de l'Isle is an adorable little restaurant in the St-Barth Isle de France hotel. The menu consists of delicious, classic French dishes. If you are a fan of salads or fish you are in luck, as these figure prominently on the menu.

Entertainment

During the day, things are really hopping in St. Barts, but as soon as the sun sets and it gets dark, the energy level comes down a notch or two. Most people head out for dinner, ending the day with a good meal. There are, however, a few bars and discotheques for those who want to dance or have a drink. Aside from these few night spots, you can also celebrate during the holidays, when lots of activities are organized. There is something for everyone, except perhaps gamblers looking to try their luck, as there are no casinos on the island.

Gustavia

Sélect
Rue France
There are a few pleasant bars in town, where you can spend a pleasant evening in a relaxing setting. One such establishment is Sélect, a friendly bar whose simple garden is an ideal place for a beer. On certain holiday nights, musicians play here live.

Bar de l'Oubli
Rue de France
Right across the street, the Bar de l'Oubli gets crowded as early as 6pm, when a young clientele starts off its evening there. The place remains full late into the night. It is an ideal place to sip a drink as night falls on Gustavia.

L'Escale
Rue Jeanne d'Arc
If you prefer somewhere with a view of the marina, try L'Escale. The lively atmosphere and rhythmic music set the mood. There is also a good selection of cocktails.

L'Ananas
Rue de l'Église
For a quieter evening, opt for the piano bar at the restaurant L'Ananas.

Repaire des Rebelles et des Émigrés
Rue de la République
This is a great place to finish your day, where you can enjoy the wonderful room looking out on the marina as well as the chic yet relaxed ambiance. There is also a pool table.

Jungle Café
Rue Jeanne d'Arc
The very pleasant Jungle Café is unquestionably the best place on the island for a night out. Its rattan furniture, arts and crafts from around the world and won-

derfully subdued lighting make it a real tropical nightspot. Patrons can also choose to sit on the terrace overlooking the marina. The establishment is frequented by people of all ages.

Carl Gustav
The bar at the Carl Gustav hotel distinguishes itself by its piano bar, where guests can enjoy listening to music in a relaxing setting.

Saint-Jean

La Créole
At La Créole you can either enjoy a simple meal at the restaurant or sip a cocktail in the casual bar. The terrace is a welcoming spot.

Eden Rock
Eden Rock is right on Saint-Jean's beach. Visitors can take full advantage of this truly fabulous spot while enjoying a drink. The place attracts a well-to-do clientele.

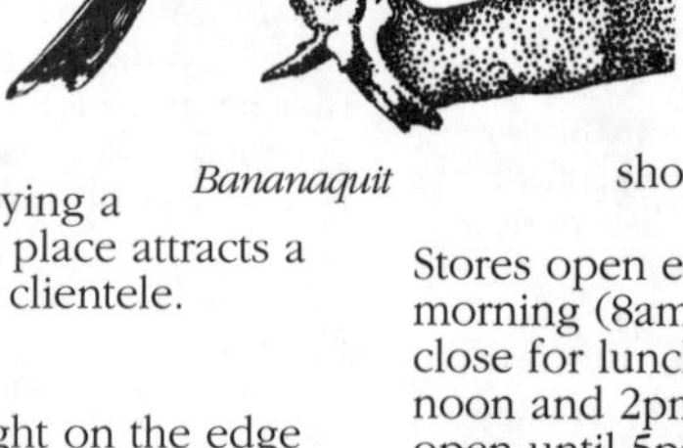

Bananaquit

Filao
Located right on the edge of the beach, the hotel Filao's bar has a magnificent view.

Grand Cul-de-Sac

El Sereno
In Anse du Grand Cul-de-Sac, the relaxed ambiance of the El Sereno hotel's bar makes it one of the most pleasant places to sip a drink and contemplate the ocean.

Shopping

Tax-free St. Barts is a veritable shopper's paradise; this pastime has become one of the most popular on the island. To better serve visitors, the island's shops are stocked with an abundance of wares of all kinds, often of good quality: jewellery, household articles, clothing, perfume, cosmetics. The majority of these shops are located in Gustavia and in Saint-Jean's shopping centres.

Stores open early in the morning (8am), and most close for lunch (between noon and 2pm), then reopen until 5pm or 6pm. They are closed on Sundays.

Gustavia

Clothing and Accessories

Beautiful garments by French and Italian designers can be purchased in chic establishments such as **Cacharel** *(Rue du Général de Gaulle)*, **Gucci** *(Rue du Bord de Mer)* and **Ralph Lauren** *(Rue Auguste Nyman)*.

For classic but relatively affordable clothes, try **Pati Séragraphie** *(Rue Schœlcher)* or **Stéphane et Bernard** *(Rue de la République)*.

Three good shops to keep in mind for lovely beach wear and swimsuits are **Calypso** *(Rue de la République)*, **Outremer** *(Rue de la République)* and **Kanelle** *(Rue du Général de Gaulle)*. The boutique **Homme de la mer** *(Rue du Général de Gaulle)* has a fine collection of beach-wear for men.

T-shirt collectors will have a field day in Gustavia. A few shops stand out from the others with their selection of tropical T-shirts: **Couleurs des Îles** *(Rue du Général de Gaulle)* and **Hookipa** *(Rue du Bord de Mer)*.

Visitors will notice people throughout the island wearing great T-shirts with the following logo: "**St. Barth West French Indies**"; these can be found in the shop of the same name on Rue de la République.

The trendiest T-shirts are probably those sold at **St. Barth d'Abord** *(Quai de la République)*. They are all adorned with a flag that once graced the ships of the island's inhabitants.

Vacationers are sure to find something at **Linnz'e** *(Rue de la France)*, which has a lovely collection of swimsuits, bikinis and sarongs.

Clémentine et Julien *(Rue du Roi Oscar II)* carries very attractive garments for children of all ages, from newborns to 14-year-olds. Pyjamas, pants, skirts, hats—everything for the little ones.

Souvenirs and Gifts

Visitors can purchase posters from **Martine Cotten** *(Rue de la République)*, who paints very charming and romantic Caribbean scenes.

For a souvenir, a statuette or some kind of decorative object, both **La Quichenotte** *(Rue du Centenaire)* and **Papayo** *(Rue du Général de Gaulle)* have beautiful collections of Creole arts and crafts.

Sailing buffs will find their heart's content at **Loulou's Marine** *(Rue de la France).*

The **Petite Maison de Marie St. Barth** *(Rue du Roi Oscar II)* is just the place for those seeking lovely presents to bring home. Household articles, dishes and bath towels as well as high-quality clothing printed with the boutique's attractive logos are just some of the items to be found here.

Jewellery

Visitors shopping for a choice bracelet, necklace or earrings can take a look at the magnificent collections at **Carat** *(Rue de la République)*, **Fabienne Miot** *(Rue de la République)*, **Cartier** *(Rue de la République)*, **Little Switzerland** *(Rue de France)* and **Oro de Sol** *(Rue de la République)*, especially if cost is not an issue. You can also let yourself be tempted by curios or Baccarat, Daum and Lalique crystal.

Those whose budgets or tastes are more inclined toward seashell or mother-of-pearl jewellery can visit the **Shell Shop** *(Rue du Général de Gaulle).*

Perfumes and Cosmetics

Visitors will find a wide range of beauty products as well as French and American perfumes in the **Chamade** *(Rue de la République)* and **Privilège** *(Rue de la République)* boutiques.

Soap, sun lotion, after-sun moisturizer, herbal shampoo, many other body lotions and more are all available at **Gustavia Santé Beauté** *(Rue du Bord de l'Eau).*

Cigars, Wine and Spirits

To stock up on cigars, fine wines and spirits, three shops should be kept in mind: **Smoke and Booze** *(Rue du Général de Gaulle)*, **La Cave** *(Quai de la République)* and, for Cuban or Dominican cigars, the **Comptoir du Cigare** *(Rue du Général de Gaulle).*

Saint-Jean

Clothing and Accessories

Shoppers looking for high-quality bathing suits and beach-wear will have much to choose from at the **Black Swan** *(Villa Créole)* boutique.

Right next door, **Surf Shop** *(Villa Créole)* also offers terrific swimsuits with more sporty cuts.

Biba Centre Commercial *(Saint-Jean shopping centre)* is yet another fine store that sells swimsuits.

For casual, classically tailored clothes, **Stéphane et Bernard** *(La Savane, facing the airport)* is a must.

Holiday-makers are sure to find attractive apparel, perfect for the island's climate, at **Morgan** *(Villa Saint-Jean)*.

Jewellery

Kornerupine *(Villa Créole)* also offers an attractive selection of seashell, silver and gold jewellery.

Groceries

You can buy most provisions at the **Match** supermarket across from the airport.

Souvenirs and Gifts

St. Barts T-shirts and beauty products, as well as a host of other quality products made on the island, can be found at **Made in Saint-Barth** *(Centre Commercial Saint-Jean)*.

Lorient

Perfume and Cosmetics

If you are looking for products more typical of St. Barts, **La Ligne de Saint-Barth** *(Route de Saline)* is an absolute must. They sell a line of beauty products made right on the premises from natural ingredients.

Groceries

There are two adjacent grocery stores in Lorient, the **Mini Mart** and **Jojo Supermarket**, both of which offer a good selection.

Glossary

GREETINGS	
Hi (casual)	*Salut*
How are you?	*Comment ça va?*
I'm fine	*Ça va bien*
Hello (during the day)	*Bonjour*
Good evening/night	*Bonsoir*
Goodbye, See you later	*Bonjour, Au revoir, à la prochaine*
Yes	*Oui*
No	*Non*
Maybe	*Peut-être*
Please	*S'il vous plaît*
Thank you	*Merci*
You're welcome	*De rien, Bienvenue*
Excuse me	*Excusez-moi*
Do you speak English?	*Parlez-vous anglais ?*
Slower, please.	*Plus lentement, s'il vous plaît.*
What is your name?	*Quel est votre nom?*
My name is...	*Je m'appelle...*
DIRECTIONS	
Is there a tourism office near here?	*Est-ce qu'il y a un bureau de tourisme près d'ici?*
There is no...	*Il n'y a pas de...,*
Where is...?	*Où est le/la ... ?*
straight ahead	*tout droit*
to the right	*à droite*
to the left	*à gauche*
beside	*à côté de*
near	*près de*
here	*ici*
there, over there	*là, là-bas*
into, inside	*à l'intérieur*
outside	*à l'extérieur*
far from	*loin de*
between	*entre*
in front of	*devant*
behind	*derrière*
GETTING AROUND	
airport	*aéroport*
on time	*à l'heure*
late	*en retard*
cancelled	*annulé*
plane	*l'avion*
car	*la voiture*
train	*le train*
boat	*le bateau*
bicycle	*la bicyclette, le vélo*

bus	*l'autobus*
train station	*la gare*
bus stop	*un arrêt d'autobus*
The bus stop, please	*l'arrêt, s'il vous plaît*
street	*rue*
avenue	*avenue*
road	*route, chemin*
highway	*autoroute*
rural route	*rang*
path, trail	*sentier*
corner	*coin*
neighbourhood	*quartier*
square	*place*
tourist office	*bureau de tourisme*
bridge	*pont*
building	*immeuble*
safe	*sécuritaire*
fast	*rapide*
baggage	*bagages*
schedule	*horaire*
one way ticket	*aller simple*
return ticket	*aller retour*
arrival	*arrivée*
return	*retour*
departure	*départ*
north	*nord*
south	*sud*
east	*est*
west	*ouest*

ACCOMMODATION

inn	*auberge*
youth hostel	*auberge de jeunesse*
bed and breakfast	*gîte*
hot water	*eau chaude*
air conditioning	*climatisation*
accommodation	*logement, hébergement*
elevator	*ascenseur*
bathroom	*toilettes, salle de bain*
bed	*lit*
breakfast	*déjeuner*
manager, owner	*gérant, propriétaire*
bedroom	*chambre*
pool	*piscine*
floor (first, second...)	*étage*
main floor	*rez-de-chaussée*
high season	*haute saison*
off season	*basse saison*
fan	*ventilateur*

TOURING	
river	*fleuve, rivière*
waterfalls	*chutes*
viewpoint	*belvedère*
hill	*colline*
garden	*jardin*
wildlife reserve	*réserve faunique*
peninsula	*péninsule, presqu'île*
south/north shore	*côte sud/nord*
town or city hall	*hôtel de ville*
court house	*palais de justice*
church	*église*
house	*maison*
manor	*manoir*
bridge	*pont*
basin	*bassin*
dam	*barrage*
workshop	*atelier*
historic site	*lieu historique*
train station	*gare*
stables	*écuries*
convent	*couvent*
door, archway, gate	*porte*
customs house	*douane*
locks	*écluses*
market	*marché*
canal	*canal*
channel	*chenal*
seaway	*voie maritime*
museum	*musée*
cemetery	*cimitière*
mill	*moulin*
windmill	*moulin à vent*
hospital	*Hôtel Dieu*
high school	*école secondaire*
lighthouse	*phare*
barn	*grange*
waterfall(s)	*chute(s)*
sandbank	*batture*
neighbourhood, region	*quartier*

NUMBERS

1	*un*	6	*six*
2	*deux*	7	*sept*
3	*trois*	8	*huit*
4	*quatre*	9	*neuf*
5	*cinq*	10	*dix*

Index

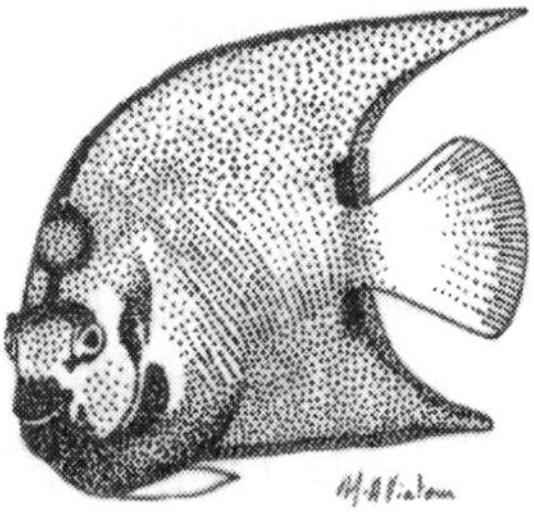

Order Form

Ulysses Travel Guides

☐ Acapulco	$14.95 CAN	$9.95 US
☐ Alberta's Best Hotels and Restaurants	$14.95 CAN	$12.95 US
☐ Arizona–Grand Canyon	$24.95 CAN	$17.95 US
☐ Atlantic Canada	$24.95 CAN	$17.95 US
☐ Beaches of Maine	$12.95 CAN	$9.95 US $10.95 US
☐ Belize	$16.95 CAN	$12.95 US
☐ Boston	$17.95 CAN	$12.95 US
☐ British Columbia's Best Hotels and Restaurants	$14.95 CAN	$12.95 US
☐ Calgary	$17.95 CAN	$12.95 US
☐ California	$29.95 CAN	$21.95 US
☐ Canada	$29.95 CAN	$21.95 US
☐ Cancún & Riviera Maya	$19.95 CAN	$14.95 US
☐ Cape Cod, Nantucket and Martha's Vineyard	$24.95 CAN	$17.95 US
☐ Cartagena (Colombia)	$12.95 CAN	$9.95 US
☐ Chicago	$19.95 CAN	$14.95 US
☐ Chile	$27.95 CAN	$17.95 US
☐ Colombia	$29.95 CAN	$21.95 US
☐ Costa Rica	$27.95 CAN	$19.95 US
☐ Cuba	$24.95 CAN	$17.95 US
☐ Dominican Republic	$24.95 CAN	$17.95 US
☐ Ecuador and Galápagos Islands	$24.95 CAN	$17.95 US
☐ El Salvador	$22.95 CAN	$14.95 US

☐ Guadalajara	$17.95 CAN	$12.95 US
☐ Guadeloupe	$24.95 CAN	$17.95 US
☐ Guatemala	$24.95 CAN	$17.95 US
☐ Havana	$16.95 CAN	$12.95 US
☐ Hawaii	$29.95 CAN	$21.95 US
☐ Honduras	$24.95 CAN	$17.95 US
☐ Huatulco–Puerto Escondido	$17.95 CAN	$12.95 US
☐ Inns and Bed & Breakfasts in Québec	$14.95 CAN	$10.95 US
☐ Islands of the Bahamas	$24.95 CAN	$17.95 US
☐ Jamaica	$24.95 CAN	$17.95 US
☐ Las Vegas	$17.95 CAN	$12.95 US
☐ Lisbon	$18.95 CAN	$13.95 US
☐ Los Angeles	$19.95 CAN	$14.95 US
☐ Los Cabos and La Paz	$14.95 CAN	$10.95 US
☐ Louisiana	$29.95 CAN	$21.95 US
☐ Martinique	$24.95 CAN	$17.95 US
☐ Miami	$9.95 CAN	$12.95 US
☐ Montréal	$19.95 CAN	$14.95 US
☐ New England	$29.95 CAN	$21.95 US
☐ New Orleans	$17.95 CAN	$12.95 US
☐ New York City	$19.95 CAN	$14.95 US
☐ Nicaragua	$24.95 CAN	$16.95 US
☐ Ontario	$27.95 CAN	$19.95US

☐ Ontario's Best Hotels and Restaurants . . . $27.95 CAN $19.95US
☐ Ottawa–Hull . . . $17.95 CAN $12.95 US
☐ Panamá . . . . . . $24.95 CAN $17.95 US
☐ Peru . . . . $27.95 CAN $19.95 US
☐ Phoenix . . . . . . $16.95 CAN $12.95 US
☐ Portugal . . . . . . $24.95 CAN $16.95 US
☐ Provence & the Côte d'Azur $29.95 CAN $21.95US
☐ Puerto Plata–Sosua . . $14.95 CAN $9.95 US
☐ Puerto Rico . . . $24.95 CAN $17.95 US
☐ Puerto Vallarta . $14.95 CAN $9.95 US
☐ Québec . . . . . . $29.95 CAN $21.95 US
☐ Québec City . . . $17.95 CAN $12.95 US
☐ San Diego . . . . $17.95 CAN $12.95 US
☐ San Francisco . . $17.95 CAN $12.95 US
☐ Seattle . . . . $17.95 CAN $12.95 US
☐ St. Lucia . . . . . . $17.95 CAN $12.95 US
☐ St. Martin–St. Barts . . . . $17.95 CAN $12.95 US
☐ Toronto . . . . . . $19.95 CAN $14.95 US
☐ Tunisia . . . . $27.95 CAN $19.95 US
☐ Vancouver . . . . $17.95 CAN $12.95 US
☐ Washington D.C. $18.95 CAN $13.95 US
☐ Western Canada $29.95 CAN $21.95 US

budget.zone

☐ Central America $14.95 CAN $10.95 US
☐ Western Canada $14.95 CAN $10.95 US

Ulysses Travel Journals

☐ Ulysses Travel Journal (Blue, Red, Green, Yellow, Sextant) . . . . $9.95 CAN $7.95 US
☐ Ulysses Travel Journal (80 Days) . . . . . $14.95 CAN $9.95 US

Ulysses Green Escapes

☐ Cross-Country Skiing and Snowshoeing . . in Ontario $22.95 CAN $16.95 US
☐ Cycling in France $22.95 CAN $16.95 US
☐ Cycling in . . . . . Ontario $22.95 CAN $16.95 US
☐ Hiking in the . . Northeastern U.S. $19.95 CAN $13.95 US
☐ Hiking in . . . . . Québec $22.95 CAN $16.95 US
☐ Hiking in . . . . . Ontario $22.95 CAN $16.95 US
☐ Ontario's Bike Paths and Rail Trails . $19.95 CAN $14.95 US

Ulysses Conversation Guides

☐ French for Better Travel .... $9.95 CAN $6.50 US

☐ Spanish for Better Travel in Latin America $9.95 CAN $6.50 US

Title	Qty	Price	Total
Name:		Subtotal	
		Shipping	$4.75CAN $3.75US
Address:		Subtotal	
		GST in Canada 7%	
		Total	
Tel:		Fax:	
E-mail:			

Payment: ☐ Cheque ☐ Visa ☐ MasterCard

Card number____________________________

Expiry date________________

Signature____

ULYSSES TRAVEL GUIDES

4176 St. Denis Street,
Montréal, Québec,
H2W 2M5
☎(514) 843-9447
Fax: (514) 843-9448

305 Madison Avenue,
Suite 1166,
New York, NY 10165

Toll-free: 1-877-542-7247
Info@ulysses.ca
www.ulyssesguides.com